The New York Times

SPRINGTIME SOLVING CROSSWORDS

The New York Times

SPRINGTIME SOLVING CROSSWORDS
75 Bright and Easy Puzzles

Edited by Will Shortz

ST. MARTIN'S GRIFFIN ≈ NEW YORK

ACROSS

1 Teenage Mutant ___ Turtles
6 Perfect school grade
11 Bar bill
14 Spring zodiac sign
15 Promote
16 When a plane is due in, for short
17 Wins a dispute
19 Some "General Hospital" roles, in brief
20 Sci-fi vehicle
21 Cry between "ready" and "go"
22 I.R.S. experts
23 Microscope part
26 Pompous pronoun
29 Clean air org.
30 Recent: Prefix
31 Pretty good
32 YouTube upload
34 Andy Warhol genre
37 "It's a mystery to me"
42 Two-front, as a Coast Guard rescue
43 Practical application
44 Italian shrimp dish
47 Blaster's buy
49 Call ___ day
50 Sob stories
53 Off-road bikes, for short
54 Cameo shape
55 Numeral at the top of grandfather clocks
56 Yonder yacht
58 "___ Misérables"
59 In romantic pursuit
64 Annoy
65 Draw forth
66 43rd president's nickname
67 Crime lab evidence
68 Satisfy, as a mortgage
69 Shuts tightly

DOWN

1 Remind too often
2 Wrath
3 Trivial complaint
4 Subject of Handel's "Messiah"
5 Beginning on
6 16th president's nickname
7 Rap artist's entourage
8 Less lofty
9 National paper
10 Home for hogs
11 Place of worship
12 When many duels were held
13 Long-eared hound
18 Make mention of
22 Bit of desert flora
23 ___ Strauss jeans
24 Grand-scale
25 Zilch
27 Optimistic feelings
28 Umpire's yell
30 Vacation resort policy, perhaps
33 Tooth covering
35 Soccer spectator's shout
36 Student of Socrates
38 Compound containing O3
39 Hang around (for)
40 "House Hunters" cable channel
41 Thumbs-up votes
44 Unemotional
45 Where to find stalactites and stalagmites
46 Fairbanks's home
48 "M*A*S*H" soft drink
51 Equip
52 So-called "white magic"
53 Put up a fuss
57 Discontinues
59 The "p" in m.p.h.
60 "Just a cotton-pickin' minute!"
61 Bout-sanctioning org.
62 Olive ___ (Popeye's sweetie)
63 W. Hemisphere alliance

by Stanley Newman

2

ACROSS

1 Band with the 22x platinum album "Back in Black"
5 Second-in-command to Captain Kirk
10 State south of Manitoba: Abbr.
14 Mythological hammer thrower
15 Bejeweled headgear
16 River to the Seine
17 Make gentle
18 Innocent ___ proven guilty
19 TV show for which Bill Cosby won three Emmys
20 Squelches early
23 Immigrant's course: Abbr.
24 Donkey
25 Ones dealing in futures?
29 Like the sound of a teakettle
32 Move so as to hear better, say
33 Took care of, as a bill
34 Got the wrinkles out
38 Mai ___
39 Capital of Latvia
40 Queen, en Español
41 Edible seaweed
42 Raptorial seabird
43 Syrup sources
44 Pseudonym of the artist Romain de Tirtoff
45 Likes a whole lot
47 Caveat ___
49 Stanley who co-directed "Singin' in the Rain"
50 Bit of song and dance, e.g.
53 "Ain't ___ shame?"
54 51-Down's talent . . . or what the circled squares represent?

59 Puzzle with a start and a finish
62 Scent
63 Once again
64 Smart ___
65 Drainage system
66 Michael of "Arrested Development"
67 Half-and-half carton, often
68 Name of eight English kings
69 Water whirled

DOWN

1 Envelope abbr.
2 Spiced Indian tea
3 Pricey bubbly
4 Lover of Troilus in a Shakespeare play
5 Gobsmack
6 Vessel of 1492
7 "#@*!" and such
8 Breaks down, in a way
9 Former "Meet the Press" host Marvin
10 "Beats me!"
11 Insult, slangily
12 Nile reptile
13 Critical
21 "___ be back!"
22 Like many items listed on eBay
26 Put on a show
27 Theater district
28 One taking potshots
29 Butter or mayo
30 Weave, shag or braids
31 Turkish "dollars"
32 Tenancy document
35 What people think of you, for short
36 Word with baby, bath or banana

37 Uptown dir. in N.Y.C.
41 Stayed with the leader
43 Computer list
46 Turn down, as a manuscript
48 Russian fighter jet
50 Say "O.K."
51 Circus performer
52 Official with a stopwatch
55 Deep cut
56 ___ a one
57 Anyone who can speak Klingon, e.g.
58 Go to and fro
59 "The Amazing Race" necessity
60 "Prince ___" ("Aladdin" song)
61 Buddhist state

by Dan Feyer

ACROSS

1 Volcano output
4 Prospects
10 Dash
14 Person with a corner ofc., maybe
15 The Scourge of God
16 Queen in "The Lion King"
17 "The Godfather" actor
18 The 21st Amendment, e.g.
19 Sting
20 Knight ___ (former newspaper group)
22 "Falcon Crest" actress
24 Awakening
26 "How ___ Your Mother"
27 Some cons
29 It might be golden
33 Final words?
36 Dockworkers' grp.
37 Allergy-afflicted dwarf
38 Car with the numeral 9 in all its model names
39 Pro baseball level . . . or a hint to 12 answers in this puzzle
41 River across the French/German border
42 Speed skater Eric who won five gold medals at the 1980 Winter Olympics
44 Location of the quadriceps
45 Enterprise captain prior to Kirk
46 Dangerous snake
47 Raspy
49 Captain of sci-fi
51 Newborn
55 Language of Cape Town
59 Antitank artillery operator, e.g.
60 Grill
61 Jungle vines
63 It may be eaten with tikka masala
64 Itch
65 Like Jimmy Kimmel and Jimmy Fallon
66 Here, in Québec
67 ___ Turing, a founding father of computer science
68 Annual event in Los Angeles
69 Summer, in Québec

DOWN

1 Capital of Ghana
2 It's said to be salubrious
3 1953 John Wayne film
4 City or lake in northern Italy
5 Repeated step
6 The Racer's Edge
7 "___ yellow ribbon . . ."
8 Singer Morissette
9 Low bow
10 Give a right to
11 ___ de Triomphe
12 Jai ___
13 Carquest competitor
21 Make dirty . . . or clean
23 ___ Lewis with the 2008 #1 hit "Bleeding Love"
25 Doozy
28 Painter Picasso
30 He loved Lucy
31 Walton who wrote "The Compleat Angler"
32 Jane of literature
33 Producer of workplace regs.
34 Bleated
35 Footnote abbr.
37 Set apart
39 Shortstop Jeter
40 Put pressure (on)
43 Inhabitant
45 New York's ___ Station
47 Fine-tuning
48 Drunkards
50 It has its moments
52 "___ Get Your Gun"
53 Boston Harbor event precipitator
54 ___ Macmillan, classmate of Harry Potter
55 Blue-green
56 Roll up, as a flag
57 Gulf of ___, arm of the Baltic
58 Room in una casa
62 "Born on the Fourth of July" setting, familiarly

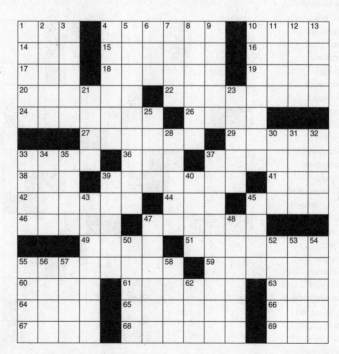

by Barry Boone

4

ACROSS

1 Scratch
4 Cries out loud
8 Football team with a blue horseshoe on its helmet
13 ___-Wan Kenobi
14 Annoying computer message
16 Nail a test
17 Stogie holder
19 Letter after eta
20 Kitchen range
21 Florida city on the Gulf
23 Singer Horne
25 "___ the Explorer" (Nickelodeon show)
26 NBC skit show since '75
27 What a TV host often reads from
30 Type
32 "The buck stops here" pres.
33 Place to hang a jacket
39 Words in an analogy
41 Thurman of Hollywood
42 Pet lovers' org.
43 Sign of alien life, some say
47 Chihuahua's bark
48 Tiny amount
49 Army do
52 HBO alternative
55 Fishing sticks
58 "I cannot tell ___"
59 Fessed up
62 Follow
65 Japanese port
66 The French Open is the only Grand Slam tournament played on this
68 "On the ___ hand . . ."
69 Completely dead, as an engine
70 "Here ___ Again" (1987 Whitesnake hit)
71 Razz
72 Projects for beavers
73 Card below a jack

DOWN

1 Footwear that may be worn with PJs
2 Somewhat
3 Verdi opera
4 Venus's sister with a tennis racket
5 "The Lord of the Rings" creature
6 Bric-a-___
7 "'Tis a pity"
8 Bit of razzing
9 Cinco + tres
10 Lecherous looks
11 Mythical giant
12 Play for time
15 Seized vehicle
18 With: Fr.
22 Clapton of rock
24 Path of a fly ball
27 Trendy
28 The Beatles' "Back in the ___"
29 Gloomy
31 Dramatic boxing results, briefly
34 "Mad Men" network
35 Soft powder
36 Astronaut's attire
37 Off-white shade
38 President whose father co-founded Yale's Skull and Bones
40 Choose (to)
44 Auto maintenance
45 One who's worshiped
46 ___ of Good Feelings
50 Chooses for office
51 Excessive lover of the grape
52 Get a move on
53 Waste maker, in a proverb
54 Midwest city whose name is a poker variety
56 All 52 cards
57 Leafy course
60 Just manages, with "out"
61 California's ___ Valley
63 Longing
64 School on the Thames
67 "Dee-lish!"

by Ian C. Livengood

ACROSS

1 Convenience for working travelers
7 The latest
11 Tire holder
14 Dog that merits "Good boy!"
15 Sore all over
16 Hoppy brew
17 Tumblers
19 Coal holder
20 Perry of "Beverly Hills 90210"
21 Flu symptom
22 Execs' degs.
23 /, to a bowler
25 Beethoven's Third
27 Frank's wife before Mia
30 N.F.L. ball carriers
31 Result of pushing too hard?
32 Tumblers
37 PC whizzes
38 Miler Sebastian
39 Crinkly sole material
41 Tumblers
44 "Would ___ to you?"
45 Bailed-out insurance co.
46 Scores for 30-Across
47 Money spent
49 Stomach problem
51 Mice, to owls
52 Marie with two Nobels
54 "Woe is me!"
58 First of three X's or O's
59 Tumblers
61 "Dig in!"
62 ___ of Man
63 Garlicky shrimp dish
64 Nonfielding A.L. players
65 Rare airline offering, nowadays
66 Repeated

DOWN

1 Lounge around
2 "___ Ben Adhem"
3 Hunt-and-___ (typing method)
4 Little squirts
5 U.K. wordsmith's ref.
6 Quick-to-erect homes
7 Born yesterday, so to speak
8 "Behold," to Caesar
9 Cabbie's query
10 The "S" in CBS: Abbr.
11 Old-fashioned pregnancy check
12 Hipbone-related
13 Good problem solvers, as a group
18 Big name in Italian fashion
22 Wisdom teeth, e.g.
24 Otto von Bismarck's realm
26 Protective part of a trunk
27 Play a role
28 Penthouse perk
29 Ones making plans
33 Unfriendly, as a greeting
34 Playfully shy
35 King's trappings
36 Went flat-out
40 Problem for lispers
42 Jingly pocket item
43 Requirement to hunt or drive
47 Made a choice
48 Dickens's ___ Heep
49 "Family Matters" dweeb
50 Big Indian
53 The Bruins' sch.
55 Long wheels
56 Mont Blanc, par exemple
57 Lost traction
59 Huck's raftmate
60 700, to Caesar

by Ed Sessa

ACROSS

1 "That's all right, ___" (lyric from Elvis's first single)
5 Knife
9 Flat floaters
14 Pearly gem
15 When said three times, a W.W. II cry
16 One who's called "the Merciful" and "the Compassionate"
17 Laugh uproariously
19 Brighter than bright
20 "Hee ___"
21 Like the word 16-Across
23 Dinner scraps
24 A Gershwin
25 Perspire mildly
27 Poindexter type
29 Guarantee
30 Crest alternative
32 Preferred way to proceed
35 "___ your request . . ."
36 Pay cashlessly
39 Blocks from the refrigerator
42 One of the Fitzgeralds
43 Poet who wrote "Heard melodies are sweet, but those unheard are sweeter"
47 Medieval infantry weapon
49 TV show set at William McKinley High School
50 Begin to grin
56 High point of a Swiss vacation?
57 Novelist Philip
58 Tulsan, e.g.
59 Mudroom item
60 "The Mill on the Floss" author
62 Boogie
64 Fruit related to cherry plums
65 Italian wine center
66 Change a sentence, say
67 ___ 500
68 Laura of "Rambling Rose"
69 Speeds (up)

DOWN

1 Punk rock concert activity
2 Jacket and tie, e.g.
3 It might give you a virus
4 Boxer with an allegiance to 16-Across
5 Fab Four name
6 Ancient Romans' wear
7 Dutch-speaking Caribbean isle
8 Dyed fabric
9 Sleazy paper
10 Permits
11 Recurrence of an old problem
12 Steak ___ (raw dish)
13 Business cheat
18 Keyboard key
22 Michael who starred in 39-Down
26 Small bag of chips, maybe
28 It always starts on the same day of the week as Sept.
31 Elevator background
32 Bud
33 Watch readout, for short
34 "So that's it!"
37 Longhorn's school, informally
38 Bud holder?
39 "The ___ File," 1965 film
40 Flower part
41 Jubilance
44 One way to serve pie
45 Mediterranean port
46 Disney's dwarfs and others
48 Came back
51 Eminem rap with the lyric "Guarantee I'll be the greatest thing you ever had"
52 Computer option
53 Wordless song: Abbr.
54 Admit
55 Onetime feminist cause, for short
61 Cough syrup meas.
63 La Méditerranée, e.g.

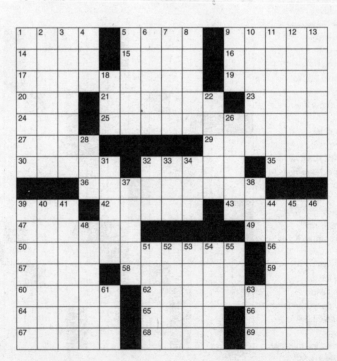

by Gary Cee

7

ACROSS

1 Fateful day for Caesar
5 All-night dance party
9 Laboratory maze runners
13 Scrabble draw
14 Completely confused
16 The "E" in Q.E.D.
17 Stratford-upon-___
18 Manicurists treat them
19 Sluggish from sedatives
20 Catch Groucho while fishing?
22 Blues player's instrument?
24 18-wheeler
25 Chaotic battles
26 French farewell
28 Falafel holders
29 Cereal that doesn't really taste like anything?
31 Period of duty
35 1930s–'40s prez
36 Beyond repair
38 Expected to arrive
39 Islamic decree
42 Wildcat that can't sit still?
45 Dances to Hawaiian music
47 Astronaut Armstrong and others
48 Burning emergency signals
50 New ___ (35-Across's program)
51 Levy paid by white-collar workers?
52 Formal wear for one's belly?
56 Cupid, to the Greeks
57 What an electric meter indicates
59 Corn bread
60 "99 Luftballons" singer
61 Fabric that's glossy on one side
62 Feudin' with, say
63 June 6, 1944
64 Left the scene
65 Numbers to be crunched

DOWN

1 Type used for emphasis: Abbr.
2 Hard-to-please celeb
3 North Carolina university
4 Submits, as a manuscript
5 Rampaged
6 Creator of the game Missile Command
7 Engine type pioneered by the Buick Special
8 Snakelike fish
9 Most sunburned
10 Got out of bed
11 Spanish finger food
12 River of Hades
15 Plus column entry
21 Easily cowed
23 "Regrettably . . ."
25 Scramble
26 Alan who played Hawkeye
27 Object thrown in a pub
28 17th-century diarist Samuel
29 Teen girl's close chum, for short
30 Laugh track sounds
32 Pastoral poem
33 Convent residents
34 Common cowboy nickname
37 Slumlord's building
40 "How about it?"
41 Otherworldly glow
43 500 sheets of paper
44 Large leaf on which a frog may repose
46 Upscale marque owned by Toyota
48 Dismissed from "The Apprentice"
49 Helmsley known as the Queen of Mean
50 Began eating
51 Look after, as a bar
52 London art gallery
53 "Animal House" party costume
54 Peck, pint or pound
55 Leather-wearing TV princess
58 Lumberjack's tool

by Patrick Berry

8

ACROSS

1. ___ the Hutt ("Return of the Jedi" villain)
6. Stuff to wear
10. Not of the clergy
14. Take a weapon from
15. Flu symptom
16. "The King and I" governess
17. Starch: a cross between ___?
20. "___ the season . . ."
21. Oscar winner for "Moonstruck"
22. Swinger who loves Jane
23. Underwire garment
24. Pre-euro Italian currency
25. Pimple: a cross between ___?
31. Sad poem
32. Pinnacle
33. Call at first base, maybe
36. Messenger ___
37. What Visine is dispensed in
38. Sunbeam
39. Apple Store offerings
41. Concerning
42. "Love Lockdown" singer West
44. Hisses: a cross between ___?
47. Word before "Boy," "Love" and "Come Back" in titles to #1 songs
48. Construction project in Genesis
49. Classic Chevy model
52. Leatherworking tools
54. No. on a college transcript
57. Beetles: a cross between ___?
60. Isaac's eldest
61. Rural road sign
62. Like helium
63. Deck hands
64. Cashless transaction
65. Seen-it-all feeling

DOWN

1. Merely
2. Not a fan of
3. Sounds in "Old MacDonald Had a Farm"
4. Reaction to a cold snap
5. "Take a hike!"
6. "Let's Get It On" singer
7. Petri dish gel
8. Choose flight instead of fight
9. Parents set them for kids
10. Prizes in early Olympics
11. 1998 animated film loosely based on "Brave New World"
12. Machu Picchu resident
13. "Come Fly With Me" lyricist Sammy
18. Title that's a homophone of 13-Down
19. Instrument on Ireland's coat of arms
23. Panhandle
24. Walked with one foot asleep, say
25. Salon treatment
26. Forearm bone
27. Get through to
28. Charles ___, hero of "A Tale of Two Cities"
29. Contempt
30. Makes at work
34. Dunaway of "Chinatown"
35. They may be lazy or wandering
37. Breaks up
40. Outbacks and Foresters
42. Alley seen on TV
43. Pump
45. Festive occasion
46. Malevolent Hindu goddess
49. "That doesn't surprise me!"
50. Mountain with a flat top
51. Distinctively shaped fruit
52. On the ocean
53. Les Nessman's station in a 1978–82 sitcom
54. Isolated valley
55. Home of former U.N. Secretary General Javier Pérez de Cuéllar
56. Italian wine region
58. Mountain ___
59. Spike TV, once

by Patrick Berry

ACROSS

1 Swiss canton
4 Good at one's job
8 Parthenon dedicatee
14 Short time to wait
15 Mast attachment
16 Brutalized
17 The cross baby was . . .
19 Places for patches
20 Brief summary
21 Book that might contain birth records
23 Homeboys
24 The cross motorist stuck at a stoplight was . . .
29 Cooks, as some vegetables
32 Doesn't give up
33 Group with revolutionary ideas
36 Author of several New Testament epistles
37 The cross man who'd been cloned was . . .
42 Pistol ___ (Oklahoma State's mascot)
43 Amassed, as debt
44 People on it get offed
47 Endless talker
52 The cross woman taking her bubble bath was . . .
55 Item in a box with seven compartments, say
56 Gettysburg general
57 Windows operating system released in 2007
58 Drift off
62 The cross aromatherapy patient was . . .
64 Lacking in knowledge
65 Exploit
66 Jimi Hendrix's "___ You Experienced?"
67 Muslim palace divisions
68 English churchyard trees
69 Naval vessel inits.

DOWN

1 Seizes unlawfully
2 Already-aired episode
3 Freezing point?
4 "Now!"
5 Object from Mars?
6 Legs and such
7 Milk carton mascot
8 Whimsical 2001 film set in Paris
9 Currency unit in the 21-Across
10 Big airport
11 "Rockaria!" band, for short
12 Just out
13 Net surfer's annoyances
18 Grp. that sends things up
22 Once-divided city
25 Stare in shock
26 Iranian coin
27 Adequately, to Li'l Abner
28 ___ modem
30 Company acquired by Verizon in 2006
31 Piteous
34 Big ___ (German W.W. I cannon)
35 What a teacher likes to hear from a pupil
37 1960s hippie event
38 James of jazz
39 Trader's option
40 Desktop item, often
41 It might make you sweat
42 21st letter
45 2001 drama whose title is taken from "Green Eggs and Ham"
46 Mounts
48 Do some political damage control
49 Guinea-___ (West African nation)
50 Lets out, maybe
51 A&E police drama set in South Florida, with "The"
53 Impart pearls of wisdom to
54 "Walk Away ___" (1966 top 10 song)
57 Ones out of service?
58 "Everybody knows that!"
59 Molecule involved in protein synthesis
60 Boston Garden legend Bobby
61 Diminutive
63 Unlovely bird sound

by Patrick Berry

10

ACROSS

1 Elba or Capri
5 Pleasant, weatherwise
10 Measure of sugar: Abbr.
14 Reduction of sugar intake, e.g.
15 Trojan War epic
16 Pro ___ (proportionately)
17 Where sad trash collectors get together?
19 Savings options for the golden yrs.
20 Stadium area
21 Cow sound
22 Mends, as socks
23 The "P" of PT boat
25 Put to good effect
27 Rock's ___ Rose
28 Where future motorists get together?
31 Architect I. M. ___
32 Fencer's sword
33 End of a student's e-mail address
34 Living off the land?
36 Smidgen
38 Org. for a Big Apple cop
42 Sir ___ McKellen
45 Snap up
48 Rousing cry at a ring
49 Where elderly picnickers get together?
53 Hair spiffer-upper
54 Holey brewing gadget
55 Spa treatment that might include two cucumber slices
57 Group of eight
58 Cries of surprise
61 Arrests
62 Soul singer Redding
63 Where stranded canoeists get together?
66 Lacking company
67 "I feel the same"
68 Gentleman's partner
69 Basic work units
70 Colorado skiing town
71 Yankee superslugger, to fans

DOWN

1 Coup leader ___ Amin
2 Extra costs of smoking and drinking
3 "Just forget about this"
4 Once-popular anesthetic
5 Offer on eBay
6 Grad
7 Chauffeur-driven auto
8 Plan, as an itinerary
9 Fabric amts.
10 Preliminary test
11 Hispanic neighborhood
12 One of four for "The Star-Spangled Banner"
13 Got a D or better
18 Wash away, as soil
22 Conked out
23 Elderly Smurf
24 Cut (off)
26 French tea
29 Spider's creation
30 Whinny
35 Sites for military flights
37 Prefix with athlete
39 Boo Boo's buddy in Jellystone Park
40 "Go right ahead"
41 Texas computer giant started in a dorm room
43 Not much
44 Stanley Cup org.
46 Furry extraterrestrial in a 1980s sitcom
47 Mel with "1,000 voices"
49 Actor Peter of "Becket"
50 Course taken by a plane or missile
51 Dining
52 Gets hitched in haste
56 French president Nicolas Sarkozy's wife
59 URL starter
60 Pump or loafer
63 "Kill Bill" co-star Thurman
64 Seemingly forever
65 Elizabethan dramatist Thomas

by Lynn Lempel

ACROSS

1. Nurses at the bar
5. "Pipe down!"
9. Derive logically
14. Bad child's stocking filler
15. Indiana/Kentucky border river
16. Sound from a stable
17. Kendrick of "Up in the Air"
18. ___ contendere
19. North Dakota city
20. Time in the title of a 1965 Wilson Pickett hit
23. Skedaddles
24. Trial fig.
25. Doo-woppers ___ Na Na
28. TV oilman-turned-private eye
33. Doll's cry
37. Aussie bounder
38. Friars Club event
39. Multiple-dwelling buildings
43. Chop finely
44. Light bulb inventor's inits.
45. Light carriage
46. Droopy-eared dog
50. Small bill
51. ___-wolf
52. Perform better than
57. Question that follows "O Brother" in film . . . and a hint to this puzzle's theme
61. Grotto isle of Italy
64. Grotto color at 61-Across
65. Java servers
66. Say "#%@!"
67. Calls upon
68. 20-0 baseball score, say
69. Ill-suited
70. "___ we forget . . ."
71. Keeps after taxes

DOWN

1. Con jobs
2. Greek column style
3. Bamboo-munching critter
4. Way of looking at things
5. ___ Kong
6. "We're in trouble!"
7. Delta deposit
8. Commotion
9. Yet to happen, at law
10. In the vicinity
11. Douglas ___
12. Cadbury confection
13. Letter before sigma
21. Suffix in poli sci
22. Ear-related prefix
25. Squirrel away
26. Minor prophet of the Old Testament
27. Prone to fidgeting
29. Prepare for combat
30. Tip of a boot
31. Scout's rider of early TV
32. ___-chef (kitchen's number two)
33. Cuban musical form
34. Bee-related
35. Parson's home
36. Circle segments
40. Vacation souvenir wear
41. Letter after sigma
42. Old biddy
47. Everyday article
48. Like some teas
49. Part of a pointillist painting
53. Driver's one-eighty
54. Severe pang
55. Glazed or powdered item
56. Gives the boot
57. Cylindrical sandwich
58. Threat-ending word
59. Razor-billed birds
60. Take five
61. CBS drama with DNA testing
62. Bristle on barley
63. Split ___

by C. W. Stewart

ACROSS

1 Hanging open
6 Cousin of an ax
10 Near Eastern V.I.P.'s
14 Doesn't have a second to lose?
15 Boutique fixture
17 Exhibited perfect braking
19 Native Nebraskan
20 Followers of nus
21 "For me? You shouldn't have . . ."
22 Nicest room on a ship, probably
27 Toward the back
28 E.T.A.'s for red-eyes
29 Here, to Henri
32 Foofaraw
35 Aloe additive?
37 "Heavens to Betsy!"
38 Cashier's error, as suggested by 17-, 22-, 47- and 58-Across?
41 Henry who made a Fortune?
42 Baby taking a bow?
43 Befuddled
44 Baton Rouge sch.
45 Peace grp. since 1948
46 "___ loves me . . ."
47 Certain loaf
54 Frigidaire competitor
56 Bumbler
57 Réunion, e.g.
58 Being frugal
63 Strongly praised
64 Goose bumps-producing, maybe
65 Funnywoman Martha
66 Actress Naldi of the silents
67 Kickoff

DOWN

1 N.A.A.C.P. part: Abbr.
2 Must, slangily
3 Something to be thrown for
4 Top 40 fare
5 Medium capacity?
6 Contribute to the mix
7 Impurity
8 Eastern state?
9 That, in Tijuana
10 "___ there yet?"
11 Handy IDs in the hood?
12 Unwanted spots
13 Kind of terrier
16 Slows down traffic, say?
18 Sign by stairs, often
23 1,000-foot-deep lake that straddles a state line
24 Many miles away
25 Game with a maximum score of 180
26 Apple offering
30 Zoo keeper?
31 Noodle product?
32 Over the ___
33 Burden
34 Number of people in a room
35 Numbered thing in the Bible
36 Friendly introduction?
37 Faster's opposite
39 Bring in
40 "Yeah, right"
45 Gerald Ford's birthplace
46 Muslim mystic
48 Theodore Roosevelt, to Eleanor
49 Man of many words?
50 Press conference component, briefly
51 Arena sections
52 Carl's wife in "Up"
53 Bowling alley button
54 On ___ with (equal to)
55 Sheet mineral
59 "There is no ___ team"
60 Name placeholder in govt. records
61 Many a Fortune profilee, for short
62 "Jeopardy!" whiz Jennings

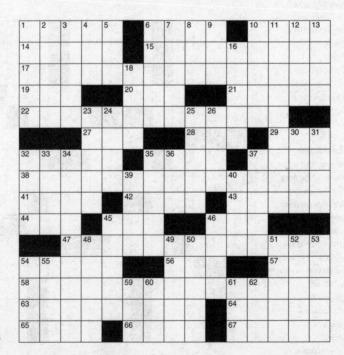

by Milo Beckman

ACROSS

1 Little argument
5 Result of a mosquito bite
9 /
14 Gas company famous for its toy trucks
15 Classic soda brand
16 Acknowledge as true, as a crime
17 Operatic solo
18 Signal, as a cab
19 Common mirage image
20 Some McDonald's burgers
23 Four-baggers: Abbr.
24 View
25 Look up to
29 It might make you go "Achoo!"
31 January 1 for the Rose Bowl, e.g.
35 Good, in Guatemala
36 Wild pig
37 ___ exhaust
38 Part of a 2005 Harry Potter title
41 "That's ___ haven't heard"
42 Paris airport
43 Be a cast member of
44 Double-___ (oboe, e.g.)
45 Bus. opposite
46 Party south of the border
47 Years on end
49 Partners for mas
50 1987 Stanley Kubrick classic
59 Lightning-fast Bolt
60 Actor Morales
61 ___ avis
62 Tooth: Prefix
63 For fear that
64 French friends
65 Heavy carts
66 Tibetan priest
67 Word that can follow the start of 20-, 38- or 50-Across

DOWN

1 N.B.A. nickname until 2011
2 Llama land
3 It's north of the Indian Ocean
4 Former Russian royal
5 "Yoo-hoo" response
6 They may stream down the cheeks
7 Chocolate-___
8 Hawaiian port
9 English biscuit served with tea
10 Items for gamblers who cheat
11 Area that may have stained-glass windows
12 Use a teaspoon in tea, e.g.
13 "Bonanza" brother
21 Pulsate painfully
22 Improperly seize
25 Despise
26 One of the Allman Brothers
27 Brawl
28 Cheating on a spouse
29 April 1 victims
30 ___ Gaga
32 Female relations
33 Not said explicitly
34 1941 chart-topper "Maria ___"
36 Drill a hole
39 Michaels of "S.N.L."
40 Mrs. Gorbachev
46 Tex-Mex wrap
48 Old Dodges
49 Ecto- or proto-ending
50 Elmer with a double-barreled shotgun
51 Manipulator
52 Actress Turner
53 Explain to
54 On an ocean voyage
55 Creature that sidles
56 ___ Sutra
57 Attorney General Holder
58 Work to do

by David Gray

14

ACROSS
1 Medicine holder
5 Walk ungracefully
11 Nick, say
14 Rights advocacy grp.
15 This point forward
16 Bon ___
17 *Area in front of a coop
19 Grand Canyon part
20 Cornfield call
21 Sea eagle
22 Some Saturns
23 *Modern school memento
28 Beatle lover
29 More clever
30 Wee, informally
31 Baseball's Blue Moon
33 O.R. figures
34 One working with checks and balances, for short
35 *Braided floor covering
37 *More than enough
41 "___ the season"
42 Play about Capote
43 Bosnian, e.g.
44 Larklike bird
47 Ore-Ida parent company
49 Language suffix
50 *Elemental parts of human nature
53 Posh
54 Letter from Homer?
55 ___ v. Wade
56 Former White House press secretary Fleischer
57 *Discover to be fibbing
62 Bee follower
63 Opposed (to)
64 Hobbling, say
65 Actors Burns and Wynn
66 Guardian Angels' toppers
67 Event with booths

DOWN
1 Hoover or Oreck, for short
2 German "I"
3 Noted 1964 convert to Islam
4 Susan of soaps
5 Character in a Beatles song
6 Wine: Prefix
7 They may be hard to find at a tearjerker
8 More loved
9 "___ Doone"
10 Knock off
11 Strand
12 Some acids
13 Composer ___-Korsakov
18 Kit ___ (chocolate bars)
22 Metal supports in skyscrapers
23 Opportunity, metaphorically
24 ___-European
25 Sticky stuff
26 When repeated, a noted panda
27 Takeback, briefly
32 Break from responsibilities, informally
34 Sovereign lands . . . or what are hidden in the answers to the six starred clues
36 "Lovely" Beatles girl
37 Baseball Hall-of-Famer Speaker
38 Actor Baldwin
39 Creator of the G.O.P. elephant
40 The "Y" in Y.S.L.
42 Like a small farm, perhaps
44 France's Élysée, for one
45 Hardened
46 Fairies
47 One getting lots of doubles and home runs, say
48 The Jewish people
51 It might be taken by a sailor
52 Author Zora ___ Hurston
57 Request inside (or outside?) a wine bar
58 Pres. when NATO was formed
59 Loosey-goosey
60 Mischief-maker
61 Fair-hiring inits.

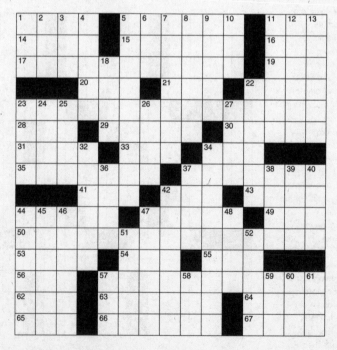

by Peter A. Collins

ACROSS

1 1960s "Bye!"
6 ___ de Boulogne (Paris park)
10 Web site with a "Buy It Now" option
14 Trip planner's aid
15 Way back when
16 Miser's cry
17 Angle symbol, in trigonometry
18 Mark in a margin
19 Have ___ (lose it)
20 Iodine in a barber's first-aid kit?
23 Ultimate degree
24 Passbook abbr.
25 Vamp Negri
26 Doofus given a pink slip?
31 Root used as a soap substitute
34 Balancing pro
35 Philosopher Mo-___
36 Dim bulb, so to speak
39 Hobby kit with a colony
42 Sans affiliation: Abbr.
43 Muff
45 Caffeine-laden nuts
46 One modifying goals?
51 Texas ___ M
52 One with a 6-yr. term
53 Tokyo, to shoguns
56 Cronus and Rhea's barbecue remains?
60 Official proceedings
61 Municipal laws: Abbr.
62 Like some checking accounts
63 Title in an Uncle Remus story
64 Unlucky number for Caesar?

65 Influence . . . and a hint to 20-, 26-, 46- and 56-Across
66 Anti-snakebite supplies, e.g.
67 Superheroes of comics
68 Well-versed

DOWN

1 Party spread
2 One of the Coens
3 Argus-eyed
4 Odds-and-ends category
5 Son of Isaac
6 Ordered (around)
7 Germane
8 Home of the Eyjafjallajökull volcano: Abbr.
9 Eighth-inning hurler, often
10 Many résumé submissions, these days
11 Like a New York/Los Angeles romance
12 In a bit
13 Bow wood
21 Results of most 100-yd. returns
22 You, to Yves
27 Serpent's home
28 Curative locale
29 Cornell of Cornell University
30 2012 Charlotte conventioneers: Abbr.
31 Sarah McLachlan hit
32 Bond that's often tax-free, for short
33 Rembrandt, notably
37 Player of a TV junkman

38 Hoopster Erving, to fans
40 End-of-fight letters
41 Predicted
44 "The Satanic Verses" novelist
47 Much of Libya
48 Mayo is part of it
49 Greets at the door
50 What might make molehills out of a mountain?
54 Willem of "Platoon"
55 Best
56 Spread unit
57 At one's fighting weight, say
58 Machu Picchu builder
59 Paving stone
60 Gym rat's "six-pack"

by Steve Salitan

ACROSS

1 Common interjection on 27-/44-Across
5 Corn, wheat or soybeans
9 Mobile downloadables
13 Ark builder
14 Amours
16 Underground part of a plant
17 Where plank-walkers end up on 27-/44-Across
20 Often-purple flowers
21 500 sheets
22 Big bird Down Under
23 "It's the ___ I can do"
25 "Hold it!," on 27-/44-Across
27 With 44-Across, annual celebration on 9/19
31 That woman
32 Yours, in Tours
33 Never, in Nuremberg
34 Gog and ___ (enemies of God, in Revelation)
36 Deep-toned woodwind
38 Bird in a "tuxedo"
40 Malevolent spirit
41 Cushion
42 Actress Swenson of "Benson"
43 Asian electronics giant
44 See 27-Across
46 Treasure on 27-/44-Across
48 Sometimes-sprained joint
49 Pretend
50 Watch sound
52 Playmate of Tinky Winky, Dipsy and Po
57 "I don't believe it!," on 27-/44-Across
60 "___ la Douce"
61 Ultimate authority
62 "The Art of Fugue" composer
63 Onetime competitor of Nair
64 Glowing gas
65 Hello, on 27-/44-Across

DOWN

1 "I've fallen . . . ___ can't get up!"
2 Surf sound
3 Sitar player Shankar
4 John ___-Davies of the "Lord of the Rings" trilogy
5 Get near to
6 Harry Potter's best friend
7 Be a foreman of
8 Onetime money in Spain
9 Curve
10 Do some investigating
11 Sonnets and haikus
12 Peacock's walk
15 1970s radical org.
18 Set, as mousse
19 Resident of Nebraska's largest city
24 Related (to)
26 ___ burger (meatless dish)
27 Key on the far left of a keyboard
28 Not much
29 Take immediate steps
30 Destiny
34 Award hung on a chain or ribbon
35 Prefix with byte
37 Immature egg cell
38 The "P" of PRNDL
39 Aye's opposite
41 Ocular inflammation also known as conjunctivitis
44 Dot-chomping character in a classic arcade game
45 What there's no "I" in
46 Place to wash up
47 Autumn hue
51 1040 org.
53 "Mamma Mia" group
54 Jacob's first wife
55 California-based oil giant
56 Like a used barbecue pit
58 Winery container
59 General on a Chinese menu

by Julian Lim

ACROSS

1 PC hearts
5 Capital ENE of Fiji
9 "Star Wars" director George
14 Mont Blanc, par exemple
15 Table salt, chemically
16 Chip away
17 Way to reduce spending
19 Broadcaster
20 Coach Parseghian
21 URL ending
22 ___ instant
23 Pre-sporting-event songs
29 Baldwin of "30 Rock"
30 Genesis mariner
31 Deli side
32 Fabergé collectible
35 River to the Caspian
37 Author Levin
38 President Taft's foreign policy
43 N.Y.C.'s Park or Lex
44 Union collections
45 "Alice" spinoff
46 Nimble-fingered
48 Long skirt
50 Malone of "Into the Wild"
54 Areas targeted for economic revitalization
58 Part of Miss Muffet's meal
59 Kitchen gadget brand
60 "Mighty ___ a Rose"
61 Director Kurosawa
63 Some vacation expenses . . . or a hint to the starts of 17-, 23-, 38- and 54-Across
66 Echolocation acronym
67 Kind of sax
68 Play opener
69 Speaks silently
70 One pitied by Mr. T
71 McJob doer

DOWN

1 Poolside enclosure
2 Mice or men
3 "This just in . . ." announcement
4 Line part: Abbr.
5 Composer Bruckner
6 Game with four "ghosts"
7 Post-O.R. stop
8 PC key near the space bar
9 Was biased
10 Heep and others
11 First wife of Julius Caesar
12 Suffix with block or cannon
13 Sun. speech
18 Prefix with friendly
22 Divided 50/50
24 Reykjavik's land: Abbr.
25 15th-century French king nicknamed "the Prudent"
26 Seniors' org.
27 Painter Chagall
28 Have influence on
33 Wander, with "about"
34 In a mood to complain
36 Follower of a chat room joke
38 Miami-___ County
39 Place for a roast
40 More than liberal
41 Very expensive
42 Voodoo charm
47 Persian Gulf capital
49 Sees through, in a way
51 Intertwine
52 On the verge of
53 Invites to enter one's home
55 Brings up
56 Heap kudos on
57 Suffix meaning "animals"
61 Balaam's beast
62 Fish in backyard pools
63 U.K. fliers
64 "Xanadu" rock grp.
65 Salary ceiling

by Daniel Raymon

ACROSS

1 Humped ox
5 Indo-European language speakers
11 Longtime Elton John label
14 "___ (So Far Away)" (1982 hit by A Flock of Seagulls)
15 Cut some more, maybe
16 "Atonement" author McEwan
17 California home of the Crystal Cathedral
19 Something that's burned
20 Morlock's counterpart in science fiction
21 It may be felt by a blackboard
23 Hums
26 California locale just south of Camp Pendleton
29 Flightless flock
30 Home ___
31 Israeli arms
32 Positive
34 Backside
37 Two out of nine?
38 California State University campus site
41 "Ere Heaven shall ___ her portals . . .": Byron
43 Guy's girl
44 Bordelaise and others
47 Traditional Christmas purchases
49 They play in front of QBs
51 Part of rock's CSNY
52 California's Sonoma County seat
55 Concise
56 Wound up
57 Shopping site
59 Ocasek of the Cars
60 Urban areas (as hinted at by the circled letters in this puzzle's grid)

66 "Naughty!"
67 Rests atop
68 "At Last" singer James
69 Urban grid: Abbr.
70 Obfuscate, in a way
71 Pringles alternative

DOWN

1 Turn one way before turning the other
2 Prohibition ___
3 Rare site during Prohibition
4 Like scuba diving
5 View from the Leaning Tower
6 Neighborhood
7 "___ out!" (shout by a 24-Down)
8 Hubbub
9 Skin care product name
10 Severe
11 Toyota Camry, e.g.
12 Collapsed
13 Ursula of "The Blue Max"
18 Trains to Wrigley
22 Sch. in Jonesboro
23 Little, in Lyon
24 See 7-Down
25 Causes of some traffic slowdowns
27 Cousins of girdles
28 Sufficient, informally
30 Thing
33 Alias
35 The Rolling Stones' "___ You"
36 ___-green
39 Puerto ___
40 Ornamental crescents
41 After a fashion
42 One who deals in rags?
45 Last of the Mohicans?
46 Sow or cow
48 Part of S.O.P.: Abbr.
50 Flintlock accessory
53 Nimble
54 Kidney secretion
55 Start of some cycles?
58 Trouble spots?
61 Japanese supercomputer maker
62 That, in Tabasco
63 Cousin ___ of 1960s TV
64 H
65 Coltrane blew it

by Peter A. Collins

ACROSS

1. One of the "hands" in the command "shake hands"
4. Result of a burst dike
9. "O.K., O.K. . . . tell me!"
14. "So that's it!"
15. Caffè ___
16. Healing plants
17. Unused parts of a cell phone plan
20. Youngster
21. Encircle
22. Stun, as with a police gun
23. British lockup
26. Wander
28. Formal meal at a table
33. "One more time!"
35. Hops kiln
36. Lab eggs
37. X-rated flick
38. Arid
39. What a soldier wears that has a serial no.
41. Any port ___ storm
42. Letters before omegas
44. Hammerin' Hank and others
45. Question that's a classic pickup line
48. Instrument for a Muse
49. La ___ Tar Pits
50. Mountain lion
53. Chemical suffixes
55. Three Wise Men
59. Death row inmate's hope
63. Finnish bath
64. Big name in printers
65. See 57-Down
66. Person who uses the "five-finger discount"
67. Medicinal amounts
68. Juice suffix

DOWN

1. Segment
2. "___, matey!"
3. Send to base on balls
4. Pop music's ___ & Eddie
5. Restroom, informally
6. Verdi opera
7. Other: Sp.
8. Actress Rebecca
9. Novelist Fleming
10. Substance in wheat flour
11. Minuscule amount
12. Flying geese formations
13. To be, in old Rome
18. American ___ (veterans' group)
19. Apple devices with earbuds
24. Wither
25. "___ to a Nightingale"
27. Impair the quality of
28. "Git!"
29. Less favorable
30. Off
31. 2007 film "___ Almighty"
32. ___-to-riches
33. Heroic tale
34. It's prohibited
38. Exigency
40. Had visions during sleep
43. Letter flourish
44. Where Nigeria is: Abbr.
46. Comic Boosler
47. Keep thinking about, with "on"
50. Whispered attention-getter
51. Salt Lake City's state
52. Hawaiian island
54. Int'l fair
56. Verdi opera
57. With 65-Across, comment that might be heard after the start of 17-, 28-, 45- or 59-Across
58. Playwright William
60. Clumsy sort
61. Iowa college
62. Young ___ (kids)

by Keith Talon

ACROSS

1 Nile bird
5 A ditz hasn't one
9 ___ Downs
14 "High Hopes" lyricist
16 Slightest amount
17 Guilty plea, say
18 Lilylike garden plant
19 It might make the nose wrinkle
20 Singer with the #1 R&B hit "I Feel for You"
22 Suffix with ox- or sulf-
23 "Paper Moon" father and daughter
24 Biscotti flavor
26 Like Batman, the Lone Ranger, etc.
29 Hagen of stage and screen
30 Japan's "way of the gods" religion
32 Eurasian duck
36 Pre-K child
37 Scam . . . or an apt title for this puzzle?
39 Useless tic-tac-toe line
40 Certain blood type, for short
42 Economist Friedman
43 Suffix with no-good
44 ___ Pieces
46 Aides: Abbr.
48 Dead Sea Scrolls ascetic
51 Grafton's "___ for Outlaw"
52 He was Sonny to Marlon Brando's Vito
56 Chilly
58 54-Down by Verdi
59 Allowed to wander, as a chicken
61 Handle the fixin's for a party, say

62 Boxer who almost upset Joe Louis in 1941
63 "I'm done!"
64 Jonas who developed a polio vaccine
65 Formerly, once

DOWN

1 "A miss ___ good . . ."
2 Sport with a birdie
3 Having no delay
4 Says "Cheese!"
5 Hypo meas.
6 Nonclerical
7 "Looks like I goofed"
8 City of central Sicily
9 Gaseous hydrocarbon
10 Sneakers brand sported by Abdul-Jabbar

11 The younger Obama girl
12 Of base 8
13 Intends
15 Fashion monogram
21 Indiana University campus site
24 Grand Theft ___
25 Upper-left key
26 Cooper cars
27 Protractor measure
28 Field goal percentages and such
31 Class for cooking, sewing, etc.
33 Priest's honorific
34 Illuminated notices above theater doors
35 Stir-fry vessels
38 Bambi's aunt
41 Welcomer at Walmart, e.g.

45 Make certain
47 Give comfort to
48 Give the heave-ho
49 Politico Palin
50 Strike down
53 Place for B-2s and B-52s: Abbr.
54 Operatic highlight
55 Dudley Do-Right's heartthrob
56 Mission conclusion?
57 Car ding
60 Yellowstone beast

by Patrick McIntyre

ACROSS

1 Foe of 71-Across in Mad magazine
4 Slaps on
9 Mass seating
13 Some round components
15 "There, there"
16 Stack server
17 Genetics-or-environment debate
20 Utensil drawer compartment
21 Like guns and dump trucks, over and over
22 Brewskis
24 Shade of blue
25 "And ___ Was," 1985 Talking Heads song
28 Decathlete's implement
30 Brute
35 Discovery Channel survival show
38 "___ Theme" (1965 soundtrack tune)
39 Piedmont wine town
40 Neighbor of St. Kitts
42 Pack down
43 Wozniak or Jobs
45 Home-seeker's decision
47 Usher in
49 ___ avis
50 Bourbon and Beale: Abbr.
51 Get too much sun
53 Standing O, say
55 Chewbacca and kin
60 Saint of Ávila
64 2004 movie featuring a clash of sci-fi species
66 ___ diagram (logic illustration)
67 Wearing a disguise, informally
68 Oz creator

69 John Lennon's "Dear ___"
70 Like some rich soil
71 Foe of 1-Across in Mad magazine

DOWN

1 Went under
2 ___ B
3 Hairy legend
4 Decreases gradually
5 Off-roader, for short
6 "Evil empire" initials
7 Our 206
8 Moves furtively
9 Falafel holder
10 Israel's Olmert
11 Sported
12 Rushed
14 Some 4WD rides
18 Opts not to be discharged

19 Word before pain or treatment
23 More cagey
25 Chart-topper
26 Rush
27 Reply to a knock
29 Young migratory fish
31 Brewery lineup
32 Many Semites
33 Full range
34 Cable TV sports awards
36 South-of-the-border cheer starter
37 Washington of jazz
41 Generalship
44 Pixieish
46 Like a windmill
48 Austin Powers foe
52 Kind of question on a survey
54 Ho-hum

55 Like moiré patterns
56 Land O'Lakes product
57 "Old MacDonald" sound
58 Popular bar game
59 Adoption advocacy org.
61 Itinerary data, briefly
62 Alternative to salad
63 Camp group
65 CD-___

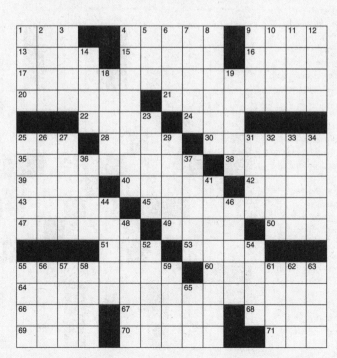

by Jeff Chen

ACROSS

1 Necklace fasteners
7 "Entourage" cable channel
10 Talks like this in "Star Wars" films he does
14 Cut the mustard
15 Dada artist Jean
16 Landed
17 Property with a mansion
18 "Fat chance, laddie"
19 Griffin who created "Wheel of Fortune"
20 Charleston is its capital
23 "All seats have been sold" sign
24 First part of a ski jump
25 Longest river in Deutschland
29 ___, Crackle and Pop
31 Trumpet's saliva-draining key
33 Skirt's edge
35 ___ Paulo, Brazil
36 Perry Mason's field
37 Kitchen cleanup cloth
41 Samuel Langhorne ___
44 Simile's center
45 Author Asquith of children's books
47 511, in old Rome
48 Not a unanimous ruling
52 Role in "Young Frankenstein"
55 "Laughing" animal
56 Biblical word with "thou"
58 Deposit, as an egg
60 Swedish liquor with memorable ads
63 Melt
66 Qty.
67 Jack the ___
68 Elvis's "___ Las Vegas"
69 Doctor's charge
70 Log-in info

71 Fix, as a cat
72 Finish
73 Eagle's grabbers

DOWN

1 Masticates
2 Focused-beam emitters
3 Takes steps in response to
4 32-card game
5 Venomous snake
6 Oktoberfest vessel
7 Abrupt finishes to phone conversations
8 Genius
9 Ready for business
10 Japanese motorcycle maker
11 Bullfight cheer
12 North, east, west or south: Abbr.
13 Off-road transport, briefly

21 Four Monopoly properties: Abbr.
22 Chicago columnist Kupcinet
26 Fashion magazine founded in France
27 ___ the Terrible
28 What literally comes from the north, east, west and south?
30 "Feels great!"
32 Informed
34 Sportscaster Albert
37 Bit of Morse code
38 Look-for-it children's game
39 Common event the day after Thanksgiving
40 Favorable sign
42 Permit for leaving a country
43 Russian fighter jet
46 Stiffly phrased

49 Sort of
50 Indenting key
51 College Web site suffix
53 One who knows the ropes
54 Earn tons of, as dough
57 Walk proudly
59 Distance units on a football field
61 Not threatened
62 German car
63 Appliances hidden in seven answers in this puzzle
64 It's rotated when doing the twist
65 Palindromic girl

by Patrick Merrell

ACROSS

1 It gets patted on the bottom
5 Tableland
9 Lead-in to boy or girl
13 Surveyor's calculation
14 Raring to go
15 Gershwin and Glass
16 Ticket usable on more than one trip
18 Basketball hoops
19 Gerund's finish
20 When repeated, cry to a vampire
21 ___ accompli
22 They make a king laugh
26 Available if needed
28 One who's supposed to be available if needed
29 End-of-list abbr.
31 Diamond cover
32 Life, in short
33 Neck cover
35 Smells bad
38 Mel who batted left and threw right
39 Become oblivious to one's surroundings
41 Completely untrained
42 Home of Arizona State University
44 Stir up, as a fire
45 Suffix with brigand
46 "___ well"
48 Alternative to .com or .org
49 Bean type
50 Like maps, iguanas and rock walls
52 Bad-mouth
54 Counterparts of dits
55 Cut with a sweeping motion
57 Greek H
58 Theater sign

59 Fast marching pace . . . or a hint to 16- and 39-Across and 10- and 24-Down
64 Dairy Queen purchase
65 Shortstop Smith who won 13 consecutive Gold Glove Awards
66 Cajole
67 Lollapalooza
68 "Butt out," briefly
69 Novelist Victor

DOWN

1 Bit of body art, for short
2 Train schedule abbr.
3 Meadow
4 Dentist's target
5 Apple on a table
6 "My word!"

7 Prefix with comic
8 Raring to go
9 Expedia calculation
10 Interval in which something is tested
11 Indian tongue
12 Helper: Abbr.
14 Artist born in 30-Down
17 WSW's opposite
22 Frilly neckwear
23 Type of type
24 Las Vegas staple
25 Nixon aide Maurice
27 ___ blanche
30 Minotaur's home
33 Former Cleveland Orchestra conductor George
34 General ___, former maker of Jell-O and Sanka
36 Rapper West

37 Promise
40 Luau instrument
43 Wall cover
47 Rarely
49 Grab
50 Anglo-___
51 Lollapalooza
53 Noshed
54 Art ___
56 "The Godfather" author
60 Drool catcher
61 Debtor's letters
62 O or Cosmo
63 Prefix with skeleton

by Susan Gelfand

24

ACROSS

1 Job for a cleanup crew
5 Fasten, in a way
11 PC "brain"
14 Place for a pavilion
15 Wild child
16 Cauldron stirrer
17 Sing-along direction
20 Masago, e.g., at a sushi bar
21 Writer Chekhov
22 Team nicknamed the Black Knights
23 Obey
25 Frank with six Oscars
28 River ferried by Charon
29 Children's game
33 Direction to an alternative musical passage
36 Become fond of
37 Fertility lab stock
40 Chase scene shout
42 "___ who?"
43 Figure of many a Mayan deity
45 Before dawn, say
47 Pursue a passion
49 Spreadsheet function
53 Neuters
54 Word missing from the answers to 17-, 23-, 29-, 40-, 47- and 62-Across
56 Worthless sort
58 One of 22 in a Krugerrand
61 "Agnus ___"
62 Do as a mentor did, say
66 Home of the Tisch Sch. of the Arts
67 First-timer
68 Play ___ (enjoy some tennis)
69 Longtime mall chain
70 Times for showers
71 Modest response to kudos

DOWN

1 Some urban transit systems
2 Urge on
3 Quick
4 Turn on the waterworks
5 Knocks for a loop
6 Oxygen ___
7 Sacramento's former ___ Arena
8 Singer whose "name" was once a symbol
9 Chaney of film
10 Dyne-centimeter
11 Game with many "points"
12 Lifeline's location
13 Like a 16-Across
18 Thole insert
19 Netanyahu's successor, 1999
24 Prefix with biology
26 The constellation Ara
27 Cultured gem
29 ___ Maria (liqueur)
30 Misanthrope, e.g.
31 Balmy time in Bordeaux
32 "Frasier" role
34 Lesley of "60 Minutes"
35 Tiny bit
37 Acapulco "eye"
38 Transportation for many a rock band
39 Demographic division
41 Whiskas eater
44 Apply to
46 Fashion monogram
48 Invite, as trouble
50 Guinness superlative
51 Richard with a much-used thumb
52 Like pretzels, typically
54 Clotho and sisters
55 Game extenders: Abbr.
56 Throw a barb at
57 "And Winter Came . . ." singer
59 Isao of the Golf Hall of Fame
60 Stir up
63 Sports stat that's best when low
64 Bribe
65 ___ chi

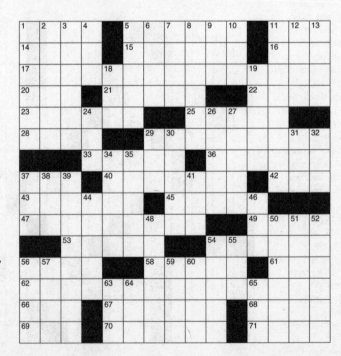

by Jim Hilger

ACROSS

1 You can stick them in your ear
6 "Planet of the ___"
10 Soft, thick lump
14 Sum
15 Leap
16 Learning by memorization
17 Bolivian capital
18 Mideast leader: Var.
19 The "a" in a.m.
20 Legendary San Francisco music/comedy club where Lenny Bruce and Woody Allen have performed
23 To the ___ degree
24 Extremity
25 Got rid of some tobacco juices, say
28 Ali Baba's magic words
35 Counterpart of hers
36 Puppeteer Lewis
37 High-end watchmaker
38 Bonus
40 Quarry, e.g.
41 Amalgamate
42 Poet/playwright Jones
43 ___ self-defense
45 Tavern
46 Bad place to live when the river rises
48 Deposit around a river's mouth
49 Road surfacing material
50 Cartoon frame
52 Everything . . . or what might cover an everything 62-Across?
60 The "A" in U.A.W.
61 Group of birds
62 Item whose varieties include the endings of 20-, 28- and 46-Across
64 Deborah of "The King and I"
65 50-50
66 Online-only publication
67 Sized up visually
68 45 or 78
69 Results of bumps to a bumper

DOWN

1 Ice cream amts.
2 Brazenly promote
3 "The Seven Year ___"
4 Mother or father
5 Caught some Z's
6 Not fully shut
7 The heart, essentially
8 Actor Jannings who won the first Best Actor Oscar
9 Wild shopping sessions
10 Junior's junior
11 Actress Anderson
12 "Beetle Bailey" bulldog
13 "___ there, done that"
21 "This isn't looking good"
22 Minimal lead in baseball
25 Bookcase part
26 Dot on a computer screen
27 Houston baseballer
29 Vatican-related
30 "Fear of Fifty" writer Jong
31 Capone henchman
32 What a murder suspect needs
33 Zinc or zirconium
34 Apply, as pressure
36 Got ready for a tongue depressor, say
39 The Greek "khalix" (pebble) for the English "calculus," e.g.
44 Ruler part
47 Examined deeply
48 Schlock
51 Fix deeply and tightly
52 Seize
53 ___ Lewis and the News
54 To live, to Lévy
55 ___ Strauss jeans
56 After-work times, in classifieds
57 Harmony
58 Opposed to, in dialect
59 Check for a landlady
63 "___ Misérables"

by Andrea Carla Michaels and Michael Blake

ACROSS

1 Hungry mouth
4 Person assisting a worship service
10 Jockey's whip
14 Lincoln, the Rail-Splitter
15 Place for a bookcase
16 Auto company whose name is Latin for "listen"
17 Title of respect
18 Longtime New York theater critic
20 Emphatic follow-up to yes or no
22 Corporate dept. that may include labs
23 Actor in 1960s TV's "77 Sunset Strip"
26 Nary a soul
29 Tropical citrus fruit
30 Fleischmann's product
32 Wilson of "Midnight in Paris"
33 Spanish king
34 Popular card game since 1954
37 Speck
38 Org. issuing many refunds
39 TV/film/stage actor once married to actress Meredith Baxter
45 Informer
48 International furniture retailer
49 Facility
50 Madame Chanel
51 Italian city famous for its cheese
53 Big dog
56 Yankee great Roger
58 Came ashore
59 Prime cooking spot
63 ___ de mer
64 "___ She Sweet"
65 "That's it for me"
66 Get along in years
67 Memo
68 Conflict waged between navies
69 ___ diem

DOWN

1 Rubber man?
2 Cut
3 In an odd manner
4 ___ Davenport, long-running "Doonesbury" character
5 Aunt ___ of "Oklahoma!"
6 Start of the third century
7 "Mazel ___!"
8 Be in charge of
9 Singer McEntire
10 Nowadays they usually have power locks and windows
11 Decrepit
12 Pindar creation
13 Fraternity letters
19 The Atlantic's Cape ___
21 Baseball stat
24 ___ pros. (court record abbr.)
25 Building extension
27 Born, in Brittany
28 Naval officer below lieut.
31 Annual theater award
34 Quaintly stylish
35 Barry Manilow's "Could ___ Magic"
36 Suffix with contradict
37 Old Mitsubishi model
39 Fondue feature
40 Alias
41 First U.S. state to abolish slavery
42 "It seems evident that . . ."
43 Alphabet trio
44 Beak
45 Motorist's guide
46 Farmland spread
47 Real young 'un
50 Piers Morgan's channel
52 Realm of beauty
54 Justice Kagan
55 Less done, as steak
57 Long-legged wader
59 Ceiling addition
60 ___ de la Plata
61 Nutritional allotment, for short
62 At once

by Bernice Gordon

ACROSS

1 Reindeer herder
5 Sprites, for instance
10 With 64-Across, 1963 Beach Boys hit
14 Lysol target
15 Fairy tale figure
16 Do some computer programming
17 1965 Beach Boys hit
20 "That doesn't bother me anymore"
21 Gumshoe
22 Gulf of ___
23 With 49-Across, 1965 Beach Boys hit
27 ___ Retreat (1970s–'80s New York City club)
30 Trouble
32 Mideast carrier
33 Fall guy?
34 1922 Physics Nobelist
35 It has feathers and flies
36 Egg: Prefix
37 Smitten one
40 Thrilla in Manila outcome
41 Wrestling victories
43 Prefix with -polis
44 Tend, as plants
46 "Cómo ___?"
47 Vote against
48 Dance accompanied by castanets
49 See 23-Across
51 Victim in Camus's "The Stranger," e.g.
52 Minor player, so to speak
53 Rich fabrics
57 1963 Beach Boys hit
61 "___ Ben Adhem" (English poem)
62 African capital
63 "It must've been something ___"
64 See 10-Across

65 "Let It Snow! Let It Snow! Let It Snow!" composer
66 Lotion ingredient

DOWN

1 Sets of points, mathematically
2 Man without parents
3 Kind of shirt named for a sport
4 One following general directions?
5 Packs away
6 Sen. Hatch
7 With 30- and 53-Down, 1964 Beach Boys hit
8 Thrilla in Manila winner
9 Lays on thick
10 Like some eaves in winter
11 Oslo's home: Abbr.
12 Year of Ronsard's "Odes"
13 Vote for
18 Sinatra topper
19 "You sure got me"
24 Nebraska river
25 Surveyor's stake, typically
26 Corrida combatant
27 Polite
28 Rich
29 Like
30 See 7-Down
31 Home of the Rock and Roll Hall of Fame
34 ___ Raton, Fla.
38 Ball club V.I.P.'s
39 Like some plays
42 Refuge
45 Neighbor of Montenegro

48 One of three literary sisters
50 Capital of the U.S.: Abbr.
51 Suffix with parliament
53 See 7-Down
54 Zest alternative
55 Outer: Prefix
56 ___-Ball
57 Choreographer Lubovitch
58 Native Nigerian
59 Overly
60 Didn't get used

by Peter A. Collins

28

ACROSS

1 Handkerchief stuffed in the mouth, e.g.
4 "The 59th Street Bridge Song (___ Groovy)" (1967 hit)
10 Start for a plant
14 Hwy.
15 Provide with the latest info
16 Friend in war
17 Giant Mel
18 Anti-abortion position
20 Cry to a horse that's the opposite of "Giddyup!"
22 Allow
23 Place to get a facial
24 Abandoned, in a way
27 Incorporate, as a picture in a blog
31 Kermit, e.g.
32 Ice cream flavor that's a synonym for "boring"
34 Up and about
36 Announced
38 Landon who lost to F.D.R. in 1936
39 Not shown in theaters
43 Suffix with plug
44 Not feral
45 2000 comedy "Me, Myself & ___"
46 Place to play foosball or Ping-Pong
49 Wall Street pessimist
50 Arcade coin
51 Satisfactory
56 Josh
58 Meadow
59 Concerning
60 Having no illusions or pretensions
65 Singer ___ King Cole
66 Little of this and that
67 Fiat
68 Big Australian bird
69 Move text around
70 Mrs. with a famous cow
71 Lo-___ screen

DOWN

1 Canine threat
2 "Casey ___ Bat"
3 Go astray
4 Wearing this is a PETA peeve
5 Afterword
6 Barely beaten
7 Christine of "Chicago Hope"
8 Hairy TV cousin
9 Fishermen cast them
10 Deli meat
11 Football's Manning
12 Rice Krispies' Snap, Crackle or Pop
13 Change from brunette to blonde, say
19 "___ sesame"
21 Heart parts
25 Doughnuts, topologically speaking
26 What you might R.S.V.P. to via a computer
28 1982 Harrison Ford sci-fi film
29 Funny DeGeneres
30 Actor Willem
33 Hubbub
34 Of ___ (somewhat)
35 Canonized fifth-century pope
36 SeaWorld whale
37 Green machine?
40 Sporty Pontiac of years past
41 Competes (for)
42 Tehran native
47 Tie again, as a necktie
48 "I'm working ___"
49 Yachtsman, e.g.
52 Come in second
53 ___ cotta
54 Box on a bowling scoresheet
55 Baby-to-be
57 Dumb ox
60 Mother of a fawn
61 Superannuated
62 Nintendo console with a remote
63 Snaky fish
64 "You there!"

by Milo Beckman

ACROSS

1 Handled, as a matter
6 Sleepaway, e.g.
10 Wood strip
14 "Er . . . um . . ."
15 Instrument heard in Sonny & Cher's "I Got You Babe"
16 Currency that replaced the drachma
17 "Spitting" snake
18 Roller coaster, e.g.
19 Rigging support
20 Bolt
23 Cousin of Muhammad
25 Sharer of an exclamation point on a keyboard
26 Locale of the Île de la Cité
27 Bolt
32 Tatum of "Paper Moon"
33 The "she" in the lyric "She walked up to me and she asked me to dance"
34 Window part
35 Unlikely to hug, say
37 Frozen dessert franchise
41 Part of the Old World
42 Wipe the slate clean
43 Bolt
47 Marble, for one
49 What "–" may mean: Abbr.
50 511, to Caesar
51 Bolt
56 Wrist/elbow connector
57 Every family has one
58 Energy
61 Toy sometimes pulled with a rope
62 Leer
63 It's a blessing
64 Half of a famous split personality
65 Unite under fire?
66 Smarts

DOWN

1 Word to an attack dog
2 ___, amas, amat . . .
3 They have homes that many people visit
4 Protective covering
5 Hot, scoring-wise
6 Pupil coverer
7 Somewhat
8 Number in statistics
9 ___ review
10 Renter
11 Foreign domestic
12 Choo-choo
13 See 24-Down
21 Like Brahms's Symphony No. 3
22 Jimmy Carter's alma mater: Abbr.
23 Famous ___ cookies
24 With 13-Down, "Stormy Weather" singer
28 Sound from a weary person sinking into a hot tub
29 ___-Kettering Institute
30 Also
31 Figure in Santa's workshop
35 Result of a fire
36 On fire
37 Play about Capote
38 1972 #1 hit for Sammy Davis Jr., with "The"
39 Vitamin whose name sounds like a bingo call
40 Mountain sighting
41 Writer James
42 Drinks that are often ladled
43 Given for a time
44 Attack, as across a boundary
45 "Absolutely!"
46 Born as
47 Snow when it's around 32°F
48 British boob tube
52 Store
53 Persuade
54 Big maker of 59-Down
55 Folk tales and such
59 Office staples, for short
60 ___-haw

by Michael Farabaugh

ACROSS
1 Holiday time, in ads
5 Detection devices
11 One way to stand
14 Bunk bed feature
15 Fester and Vanya
16 Shipment to a smeltery
17 Physical therapist's assignment?
19 Postal worker's circuit: Abbr.
20 Gossip, to an Aussie
21 Friend of François
22 Engaged
23 The Forbidden City
24 Blackened seafood?
26 Some small power supplies
27 Facilities, informally
29 Lift up
30 La ___ Tar Pits
32 Kind of arrest
36 Castaway's day in court?
40 Enter slowly
41 Spread selection
43 Mete out
46 It may come in a blanket
48 Bionic part of the Bionic Woman
49 Lure for Popeye's sweetie?
53 ___ Kea
55 After midnight, say
56 "Go on . . ."
57 Maliciously done
58 CPR pro
59 Choosing between pounds and kilos?
61 Funny Charlotte
62 Hang back
63 Uncool
64 Georgia, once: Abbr.
65 Customary practices
66 Hydrocarbon suffixes

DOWN
1 Medical dept. room
2 Exotic dancer executed in 1917
3 Homes for drones
4 Food-stains-on-shirt sorts
5 River to the Rhine
6 Whatever amount
7 1983 Mr. T comedy
8 1836 siege site
9 Frankincense or myrrh
10 GPS heading
11 Wife of Brutus
12 iTunes search category
13 Chew on a baby toy, say
18 Thunder sound
22 Result of a '55 union merger
24 Dance around
25 Information for an oenologist
28 Reason to use Retin-A
31 Dinette spot
33 Union ___
34 Headache for a snow shoveler
35 "Give ___ thought!"
37 Johnson of "Laugh-In"
38 Like Unalaska
39 1989 movie featuring principal Joe Clark
42 Good sources of vitamin C
43 Many I.M. recipients
44 Wool-yielding pack animals
45 Runt's group
47 Auto financing org., formerly
50 Causes of ruin
51 Man's feminine side
52 Med-alert bracelet, e.g.
54 Shackle site
57 Standings column
59 Neighbor of Braz.
60 Eskimo ___

by Kelsey Blakley

ACROSS

1 Ice cream utensil
6 Sea creature that moves sideways
10 "But wait! There's more . . ."
14 Cuban "line" dance
15 Lasso
16 Italian "bye"
17 Crowd sounds
18 Baldwin of "30 Rock"
19 Bullets
20 Buffalo wings or bruschetta, e.g.
23 Kid's "shooter" projectile
24 Formula ___ racing
25 Overly
26 Kanye West's genre
28 "E" on a baseball scoreboard
30 Sylvania product
31 Rightmost number on a grandfather clock
32 Dish under a teacup
34 High point
35 Pittsburgh Pirates hero of the 1960 World Series
39 Perry with the 1956 #1 hit "Hot Diggity"
40 Winners' opposites
41 Auto additive brand
42 Hole-punching tools
44 Swung and missed
48 Equal: Prefix
49 W. Hemisphere alliance
50 Allow
51 "___ Baba and the 40 Thieves"
52 Music source on many an old fairground
56 Western writer Grey
57 Heading into overtime
58 Source of amber

59 ___-European languages
60 Prefix with potent or present
61 Ridiculous
62 "No bid"
63 Noble gas
64 Weasel family member

DOWN

1 Predicament
2 "The Last of the Mohicans" author
3 Commensurate (with)
4 Shrek, for one
5 Rustic
6 Hula hoops in the 1950s, e.g.
7 Part to play
8 Camera openings
9 "Take a chill pill!"
10 Military sch.
11 Verse often beginning "There once was a . . ."
12 "Spider-Man" series director
13 Tic-tac-toe victory
21 All together
22 Burgle
27 Baked dessert
29 Norway's capital
30 Jeff who founded Amazon.com
33 Gives teams a short break
34 Professional org.
35 Neighbor of South Africa
36 Seizes, as a car
37 Direct elsewhere
38 Handel's "Messiah," e.g.
39 CBS forensic series

42 Time Warner spinoff of '09
43 Serve attentively
45 Pesters
46 Jerry's ex on "Seinfeld"
47 Supper
50 Ushered
53 Old-fashioned Speed Wagons
54 Greek philosopher known for paradoxes
55 Landlord's due
56 Nothing . . . or a hint to what's hidden in 20-, 35- and 52-Across

by Stan Newman

ACROSS

1 Cut down, as a photo
5 Big Apple?
9 Like many bathroom floors
14 Poland's Walesa
15 It gets hammered
16 Rub out
17 Brainstorm
18 Be rewarded for a pious life, as the devout believe
20 Abyss
22 Shipping container
23 Stereotypical sitcom greeting
26 Hypotheticals
29 U.F.O. crew
30 Roman "I"
31 Satellite-based car option
33 Former Japanese capital
35 "The Flintstones" pet
36 Castle on the Thames
41 Doll call
42 Spanish finger food
43 A girl was from there in a 1964 hit song
47 His big day is in June
48 Rx watchdog
51 Finger count
52 Pet store purchase
55 Big, big, big
56 Aired again
57 Invisible writing on a computer screen . . . or a component of 18-, 23-, 36- and 52-Across?
62 All's counterpart
63 "Doe, ___ . . ."
64 Les États-___
65 Puts on
66 Chinese restaurant request
67 Force unit
68 Apt rhyme of "aahs"

DOWN

1 Overused expression
2 In very high demand
3 "___ Eleven"
4 Developmental period
5 Suffix with seem or teem
6 Chinese chairman
7 Gee follower
8 Laundry brand
9 Be on the brink of toppling
10 "Dies ___"
11 Restroom, informally
12 WNW's opposite
13 Room for trophies, maybe
19 Soccer great Mia
21 "Balderdash!"
24 Inventor Sikorsky
25 Mr. ___, Japanese sleuth
26 Peculiar: Prefix
27 Neighbor of a Swede
28 ___ Canals
32 Tacks on
33 Skater Michelle
34 Frequently, to a bard
36 Mending aid
37 Muscat's land
38 Disney dog
39 Memorable 1995 hurricane with a gem of a name?
40 Low point
41 Cambridge univ.
44 Anita of "La Dolce Vita"
45 Appearance
46 Available for breeding
48 Farcical 1960s sitcom with the Indian character Roaring Chicken
49 Troi on "Star Trek: T.N.G."
50 "Gunsmoke" star James
53 Minuscule
54 Minds, as a fire
55 Laudatory poems
57 Solo of "Star Wars"
58 Vow at an altar
59 Those people, in Brooklyn
60 Mark, as a ballot
61 Syllable after 6-Down

by David Steinberg

ACROSS

1 "Big Brother" host Julie
5 Milky Way maker
9 "Oh, get off it!"
14 "The Godfather" score composer Nino
15 Riding on
16 Toothpaste brand once advertised with Bucky Beaver
17 "___ framed!"
18 Org. with Spartans and Trojans
19 Drug that treats panic attacks
20 M/C Hammer?
23 Verdi's "___ tu"
24 ___ in queen
25 Raking in
29 Closing bid?
31 Suspense novelist Hoag
33 ___ de guerre
34 Literally, "reign" in Hindi
36 Like Mendeleev's table
39 W/C Fields?
43 Former Ford minivan
44 Risk damnation
45 ___ tough spot
46 Mlle., across the Pyrenees
48 Summer camp shelter
52 Have the blahs
55 Emergency contact, often: Abbr.
57 Whichever
58 L/L Bean?
61 "Oops!"
64 Sac flies produce them
65 "___ be in England": Browning
66 Big Apple mayor before Koch
67 "Outta my way!"

68 Jockey's handful
69 "You're killin' me!"
70 Goes with
71 Brouhahas

DOWN

1 Yalta's locale
2 Stooge surname
3 List ender
4 Pelé's org.
5 Powerful ray
6 For neither profit nor loss
7 Have a hearty laugh
8 Sci-fi travelers
9 Studio behind "Up" and "Wall-E"
10 Engender
11 Chinese dynasty name
12 Santa ___ winds
13 You might put your stamp on it

21 Comes to
22 Scottish landowners
26 Intro to Chinese?
27 Film ___
28 Yukons, e.g.
30 Hence
32 Not connected
35 Tea in Boston Harbor, once
37 Yule decoration
38 A Chaplin
39 Ragamuffin
40 Russo of film
41 "Of wrath," in a hymn title
42 Sail supports
47 Hit it big
49 Took a dip
50 Ab ___ (from the start)
51 L'eggs wares
53 Andean wool source

54 First Catholic vice president of the U.S.
56 Someone ___ (another's)
59 "An ill wind . . ." instrument
60 Director Ephron
61 Deg. held by George W. Bush
62 Tree with cones
63 Kapow!

by Michael Black

ACROSS

1 With 69-Across where to find the ends of 17-, 22-, 32-, 43-, 54- and 61-Across
5 Organization for the supersmart
10 ___-in-the-blank
14 Most eligible for military service
15 State in NE India
16 Not working
17 Q-tip, e.g.
19 Hall-of-Famer Musial
20 Whole ___ and caboodle
21 Tetley product
22 It points to the minutes
24 Terse four-star review
27 Danish toy blocks
28 Prefix with plunk or plop
29 French notions
32 Presidential candidate's #2
36 Letter after chi
39 The Bard of ___ (Shakespeare)
40 Lifeless
41 Arkin of Hollywood
42 Part of the head that moves when you talk
43 Excellent, slangily
45 Snapshot
46 007 creator Fleming
47 Reproductive part of a fungus
50 Tire-changing group at a Nascar race
54 Sticky stuff on a baseball bat
57 Middling grade
58 ___ Newton (Nabisco treat)
60 W.W. II foe, with "the"
61 Condiment that's O.K. for observant Jews
64 Hysterically funny sort
65 Letter-shaped construction piece
66 Folkie Guthrie
67 Casino game with numbers
68 Slender amphibians
69 See 1-Across

DOWN

1 Sell at a pawnshop
2 How French fries are fried
3 Become friendly with
4 Dr. Seuss's "The Cat in the ___"
5 Like a lion or horse
6 Piece of French writing
7 Australian state whose capital is Sydney: Abbr.
8 Volvo rival
9 Prefix with dextrous
10 Uses a rod and reel
11 Item on a dog collar
12 Grassy plain of the Southwest
13 Gives for a time
18 Onetime "S.N.L." regular Cheri
23 Great happiness
25 ___ diagram (logic tool)
26 1994 Jean-Claude Van Damme sci-fi film
30 Unlit
31 Suffix with Rock
32 British rule in colonial India
33 The Cavaliers of the A.C.C.
34 Actor Robert De ___
35 Pesky insect
36 Airline ticket cost
37 Holder of a squid's 38-Down
38 It's held in a squid's 37-Down
41 Slightly open
43 Guitarist Atkins
44 Kitchen gadget for processing potatoes
45 Magician's cry
47 Start of a fire
48 Mischievous fairy
49 Weekly satirical paper, with "The"
51 Instant-messaging program for Macs
52 Swarms (with)
53 Cather who wrote "O Pioneers!"
55 Similar (to)
56 Judge's attire
59 Old Pontiac muscle cars
62 Make clothes
63 Carrier to Oslo

by Ian Livengood

ACROSS

1 One of the Pleiades
5 Q.: When is a door not a door? A.: When it's ___
9 Pickpocket, e.g.
14 ID in a library vol.
15 Dunce cap shape
16 Three-wheeled Asian cab
17 "Peanuts" figure . . . or some fabulous fall soup?
20 "For rent"
21 Figure in academia
22 Nein : German :: ___ : Russian
23 Subway turners
25 Much-derided 1980s-'90s car
27 Calif. setting for "Stand and Deliver"
30 Words to swear by
34 Off-road wheels, for short
36 Rhyme scheme for Frost's "Stopping By Woods on a Snowy Evening"
38 Onion-flavored roll
39 Early 1970s dance . . . or some smelly soup?
43 Kenyan tribesman
44 Suffix with opal
45 Key to get out of a jam?
46 At a chop shop, perhaps
48 Tennis's Graf
51 Exam for an aspiring Esq.
53 Ray of "GoodFellas"
56 Ways to the Web: Abbr.
59 It may be put on a pedestal
62 Gloomy, in verse
63 Nickname for snowboarder Shaun White . . . or some airborne soup?
66 Paddled craft
67 Canceled
68 Old camera settings, for short
69 Many-headed challenge for Hercules
70 Like flicks seen without special glasses
71 Instrument played with a plectrum

DOWN

1 Baseball gloves
2 "Give it ___!" ("Try!")
3 "Yes, if you ask me"
4 German chancellor Merkel
5 Score 100% on
6 "The Grapes of Wrath" family name
7 The "a" in a.m.
8 Compensate for loss
9 Channel for old films
10 Like a swinging pendulum, say
11 "Eww! Gross!"
12 "Night" author Wiesel
13 Helvetica, e.g.
18 Hwys.
19 "One" on a penny
24 Lee of Marvel Comics
26 Mongolian desert
28 Okeechobee, e.g.
29 Chasm
31 "Calm down!"
32 Shouts at a fútbol game
33 Harmony
34 $20 dispensers
35 "What's ___?"
37 No. at a brokerage
40 Becomes smitten by
41 Sometimes-illegal turns, in slang
42 Dog command
47 The Midshipmen
49 Relative of Rex
50 Not casual
52 Corrupt
54 One of a Turkic people
55 Got out of bed
56 Allergic reaction
57 One-horse carriage
58 Be in limbo
60 Author C. P. ___
61 Frozen waffle brand
64 Grazing ground
65 Thomas Mann's "Der ___ in Venedig"

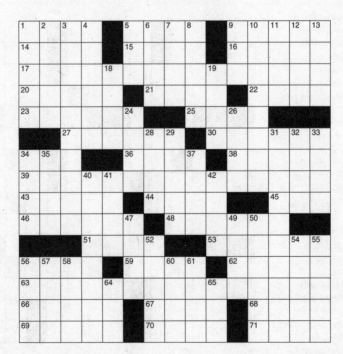

by Tony Orbach

36

ACROSS

1 Coach Ewbank who led the Jets to a Super Bowl championship
5 Sturdy mountain climber?
9 English derby site
14 Pac-12 team
15 Circular dance
16 Iroquoian people
17 Place for a sweater?
19 Composer Stravinsky and others
20 A Mexican might sleep under it
21 Totally wrong
22 "Peer Gynt" mother
23 La ___ Tar Pits
24 Sheets for scribbling
29 30- or 60-second spot
33 Three, in Rome
34 Mideast moguls
35 Not just mislead
36 Pocahontas's husband
38 Hogwash
39 When a right turn may be allowed
40 "You have my word on it"
41 Suitor
43 Certain fraternity man, informally
44 Antifur org.
45 Ice cream holder
47 ". . . or so ___ say"
49 "A New World Record" grp.
50 Put down
53 Beau
58 Full-bosomed
59 Fairway clubs . . . or a hint to the starts of the answers to 17-, 24- and 45-Across and 10- and 37-Down

60 "The Surrender of ___" (Diego Velázquez painting)
61 Whitaker's Oscar-winning role
62 "Zip-___-Doo-Dah"
63 Poe's middle name
64 Root beer brand
65 King with the immortal line "Who is it that can tell me who I am?"

DOWN

1 Scaredy-cat
2 Outside: Prefix
3 K-6 sch. designation
4 Entreaty to Bo-Peep
5 Earlyish teatime
6 Uncouth sort
7 Suffix with buck
8 Bump in bumper cars, maybe
9 Rat in "Ratatouille"
10 Playground lingo
11 Possible cause of school cancellation
12 Storybook character
13 Superlative adverb
18 Emma of "The Avengers"
21 Music sheet abbr.
23 Annual city-magazine theme
24 "Peanuts," for one
25 "Gladiator" star
26 Like a candle night after night, say
27 Breathing space
28 90 is a pretty high one
30 Left-hand page
31 Used the dining room

32 "Gunsmoke" setting, informally
35 Legendary siren of the Rhine
37 Fizzless drink
42 High dice rolls
45 Tie the knot
46 O.K. place?
48 Mr. Universe, e.g.
50 "Fernando" group
51 Small knot
52 Figure skater's leap
53 Succotash bean
54 "Amores" poet
55 Presage
56 Fit for service
57 River of Flanders
59 Goldfish swallowing in the 1920s, e.g.

by Elizabeth C. Gorski

ACROSS

1 Transact business on the Internet
6 TV/radio host John
10 Turkey club?
14 Travelers alternative
15 Toss in a chip
16 Touched down
17 Tricky driving condition
18 Tax-exempt educ. groups
19 Times Roman, for one
20 Traditional use for henna
23 Tackle-to-mast rope on a ship
24 Tiny bit
25 Typist's key: Abbr.
28 Transmitter of waves
31 Train stop: Abbr.
34 Tear-gassing cause
36 Tevye's "good"
37 The Beatles' meter maid and others
39 Team in the A.F.C. South
43 Tallow sources
44 To the ___ degree
45 Trouble with a lid?
46 Time period on a financial stmt.
47 Takes a step toward biting?
51 Took a chair
52 Trap or record preceder
53 Teleflora competitor
55 Tilt-boarding
63 Techie's address starter?
64 Topic lead-in
65 Take as a given
66 The U.N.'s Kofi ___ Annan
67 Tranquilizer gun projectile
68 Two-color horse
69 Tensed
70 Terminal approximations: Abbr.
71 Towel ends?

DOWN

1 Toward sunrise
2 The "T" of TV
3 "Time to rise!" ("Up and ___!")
4 Tending to bungle things
5 Tito Jackson's sister
6 Toledo tidbit
7 Theater's ___'acte
8 Take the night off from partying, say
9 "The Ten Commandments" star
10 Three-country agreement of '94
11 Tons
12 Two-time All-Star Martinez
13 "The Touch of Your Hand" lyricist Harbach
21 Tears
22 Tempest game maker
25 Trying to look cultured
26 Title for Sulu on "Star Trek": Abbr.
27 Tempered, with "down"
29 Talking-___ (scoldings)
30 Track meet component
31 TDs and interceptions
32 Tucker with the #1 country hit "Here's Some Love"
33 Thing of value
35 "The Closer" airer
38 T.G.I.F. part
40 "Terminal Bliss" actress Chandler
41 Third-person ending of old
42 Thug's crime, often
48 TD Waterhouse online competitor
49 Torments
50 Treeless tract
52 Time-honored Irish cleric, for short
54 Tout ___ (straight ahead: Fr.)
55 To the extent
56 "Tell Mama" singer James
57 Traitor's rebuke
58 Tomás's "other"
59 Tykes
60 "This ___ what I expected"
61 TV's Nick at ___
62 "Three deuces and a four-speed" cars of old

by Paul Guttormsson

38

ACROSS

1 Lost-and-found containers
5 It has ringers on its team
9 Brown shade
14 "Got it"
15 Sauce brand
16 Subway station sight
17 Like a sunken treasure?
20 Third of December?
21 Grp. with the platinum record "A New World Record"
22 Systems of principles
23 Ice cream flavor, briefly
26 Secretary on "The Office"
28 High place near Aberdeen?
34 One in custody
35 Breakfast cupful
36 Like most bathrooms
37 Spanish bear
38 "The Wizard of Oz" weather event
41 Eastern V.I.P.
42 "Amazing!"
44 One fawning
45 Gift tag word
46 Restraints for writer Flagg?
50 James who sang "A Sunday Kind of Love"
51 Like some textbooks
52 Complain
55 Grecian art object
57 Creepy
61 Cooking instruction hinting at this puzzle's theme?
65 Thingy
66 A.L. or N.L. division
67 ___-a-brac
68 Look of superiority

69 Cry from Charlie Brown
70 When sung three times, part of a Beatles refrain

DOWN

1 Places for double dribbles?
2 Golfer Aoki
3 Hasbro product
4 Not yet paid for, as a mailed package
5 Shot put's path
6 Kilmer of "Real Genius"
7 Kind of arch
8 Centers
9 Consume
10 Tablets site
11 Partner of pieces
12 Part of 51-Across: Abbr.

13 Some wines
18 Number after sieben
19 Honker
24 Eight: Prefix
25 Singer with a Best Actress Oscar
27 Loving
28 Olympic skater Cohen
29 Bonk
30 2008 Beijing Olympics mascot
31 Irish county north of Limerick
32 Building set
33 Mild cheese
34 Pound sound
38 Dweeb
39 Super-duper
40 25%-off price, e.g.
43 What Shakira or 25-Down goes by

45 Passes quickly
47 French CD holder
48 "Silas ___"
49 Julia Child, for one
52 High-performance wheels
53 Thor's father
54 Wood shaper
56 Org. with Divisions I, II and III
58 Exceptional
59 Pelvic bones
60 Mark permanently
62 ___ favor
63 Pres. initials
64 Periods of extra mins.

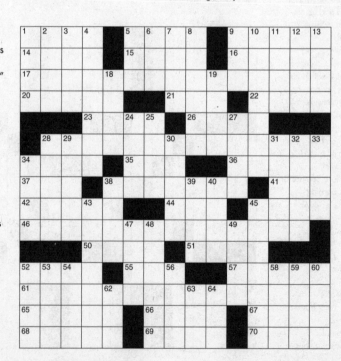

by Michael Torch

ACROSS

1 Limerick or sonnet
5 "Shut yo' mouth!"
9 Sales talk
14 Jai ___
15 Solo for Pavarotti
16 Commie
17 Use of a corporate jet, say
18 Pepper grinder
19 Heavenly harp player
20 Green Berets
23 Pest attracted to light
24 Volcanic spew
25 Words before serious, ready or listening
28 Fill all the way
30 The Peacock Network
33 Frenzied state
35 Mrs. Dithers in "Blondie"
36 Brings up
37 "Everybody Hurts" band
38 Revolutionary War hero John Paul ___
39 Las Vegas figures
40 Out-of-studio TV broadcast
42 Opposite of NNW
43 First, second, third or home
44 Nuclear experiments, for short
45 ___ Lanka
46 ___ monster
47 Popular date time . . . or a phrase that can precede the starts of 20-, 33- and 40- Across
53 Chinese province where Mao was born
54 Spain's longest river
55 Hoity-toity manners

57 Bandleader Shaw
58 Jesus of the 1960s Giants
59 It's just a thought
60 "Project Runway" host Klum
61 Take a breather
62 Requirement

DOWN

1 Soft food for babies
2 Cheers at a fútbol match
3 Dodge City lawman Wyatt
4 Portrayer of Austin Powers, "international man of mystery"
5 Chew the scenery
6 Dickens's ___ Heep
7 Spot for a pot
8 Two quarters

9 Few and far between
10 Tiny bit of salt
11 William who wrote "The Dark at the Top of the Stairs"
12 Manages, with "out"
13 Twitter titter
21 Operator of the largest brewery facility in the world
22 "Ye gods!," for one
25 Hairstyles of Sly and the Family Stone
26 Swamp plants
27 Escape, as arrest
28 Jobs in Silicon Valley
29 Pinnacle
30 Forbidden acts
31 QB Favre
32 Assignments for Sam Spade

34 Colored part of the eye
35 "Say what?"
38 Martial arts champion-turned-film star
40 Lion's home
41 Certain game cancellation
43 Pacific sultanate
45 Unflashy
46 Pita sandwiches
47 "My pleasure!"
48 Prefix with knock
49 "___ Abby"
50 Up to the task
51 Enroll in a witness protection program, say
52 Apple or maple
53 "When pigs fly!"
56 Down in the dumps

by Randall J. Hartman

ACROSS
1 Think about
7 Rock's Steely ___
10 Pentagon V.I.P.'s: Abbr.
14 Kind of reasoning, after "a"
15 Ginger ___
16 Help in wrongdoing
17 Entertainment you might have a hand in?
19 "Encore!"
20 Meat slice on the highest shelf?
22 Class with crayons
25 Scotland's Firth of ___
26 Trail user
27 Advertising sheet blowing in the wind?
32 Like presses ready for printing
33 It has feet in a line
34 Droop
37 Sir Anthony formerly of 10 Downing Street
38 Made thinner
40 Carry on
41 Oui's opposite
42 ___ Cooper (car)
43 English county
44 Curly lock tints?
47 Grove components
50 Big ___
51 Buttonless shirt
52 Dribble from an icicle?
57 Series finale, in brief
58 Nor'easters, often
62 Ocean motion
63 Be under par
64 Keyless
65 Broke ground?
66 QB pickups: Abbr.
67 ___ public

DOWN
1 Very, very soft, in music
2 Okla. school
3 Quick drink
4 L-___ (Parkinson's treatment)
5 Put up
6 Mass, e.g.
7 Author Roald
8 Lily of Africa
9 Colorful amphibian
10 Chess ploy
11 Something to read on a Kindle
12 Chutzpah
13 Manage the helm
18 Eye sore
21 Sound before "Your fly is open"
22 "The X-Files" subject
23 Sonata movement
24 Coin at an arcade
28 When doubled, a breath freshener
29 When to celebrate Earth Day
30 Axis, once
31 Was ahead
34 Nicholas or Patrick
35 Share an opinion
36 Fliers in V's
38 Wrestler's goal
39 Director Lee
40 Question of identity
42 Hit's opposite
43 Feature of a fugue
44 Staggered
45 Big game hunter?
46 Resident of Oklahoma's second-largest city
47 Canines, e.g.
48 Two to one or three to one
49 Skirt
53 Heavy cart
54 A.T.F. agents' activity
55 Removes a squeak from
56 Driver's nonverbal "hello"
59 Cellular stuff
60 "Striving to better, oft we ___ what's well": Shak.
61 Like a fox

by Mary Ellen Uthlaut

ACROSS

1 Prefix with bucks
5 iPhone user's purchase
8 Wings it
14 Came to rest
15 Pot-au-___ (French stew)
16 Sign near roadwork, maybe
17 Flashy display
19 "Water that moves you" sloganeer
20 Org. in "Burn After Reading"
21 Brand with an iconic cowboy
23 Where pastrami may be put
25 Golf's ___ Pak
26 Toss high up
30 Passover meals
32 Dutch-based financial giant
34 Test for Ph.D. wannabes
35 Having a razor injury, say
38 Like Rod Serling tales
40 Asleep . . . or a hint to this puzzle's theme
43 La ___ (San Diego area)
44 Patron of sailors
45 Nile slitherer
46 Matchsticks game
48 Marks up or down, perhaps
52 Rock trio known for its bearded members
54 "This just in . . ." fare
57 Earth, in sci-fi
58 Copycat
61 Element with the shortest name
62 Tested, as on "The $64,000 Question"

65 1892 Kipling poem
67 "Key Largo" actress
68 Prefix with dermis
69 He sang about Alice's restaurant
70 Iced rum cocktail that's stirred with a stick
71 Mr. ___ (old whodunit game)
72 Orbison and Bean

DOWN

1 Imelda, the shoe lover
2 "Seinfeld" gal
3 Giblets component
4 7-Eleven convenience
5 Shaving lotion brand
6 Compote fruits
7 You're doing one
8 Juxtapose

9 Snookums
10 Maj.'s superior
11 Paper in a poker pot
12 Caffeine-induced state, slangily
13 Eastern honorific
18 Like apple pie, in a saying
22 Game with a dummy
24 1983 Streisand title role
27 Big brute
28 Bad hair day problem
29 Kicker's aid
31 Coll., e.g.
33 Euclid's subject
36 Destiny
37 Otoscope user, for short
39 Gush on stage
40 Part of COLA

41 Bowser's bowlful
42 Camera type, briefly
43 Newport festival music
47 Out of gear
49 Conductor Toscanini
50 Yellowstone sighting
51 Some plasma TVs
53 Zest
55 Nilla cookie
56 Dimwit
59 "Momma" cartoonist Lazarus
60 Harriet's mate
62 Eli and Peyton Manning, for two: Abbr.
63 Motor City labor org.
64 Here, to Henri
66 Collect-all-the-cards game

by Tracy Gray

ACROSS

1 Homes for hens
6 Scrapes (out)
10 Sarcastic exclamation
14 Sneeze sound
15 Converse
16 Pixar's "Finding ___," 2003
17 "I'll be through in a minute"
19 Recipe direction
20 See 38-Across
21 Game show group
22 Ending for a female Smurf
23 Puts into law
25 Settle, as a debt
27 Owls' cries
30 Girl who plays football, perhaps
33 Response to "Are too!"
36 ___ salts
38 With 20-Across, just for fun
39 Part of a shoelace tie
40 Word that can precede the starts of 17- and 62-Across and 11- and 35-Down
41 Boat loading area
42 Fliers of U.F.O.'s
43 Barton of the Red Cross
44 Erases, as a computer's memory
45 Mount Everest guide
47 Big name in printers
49 "Pride and Prejudice" beau
51 Like Papa Bear's porridge, to Goldilocks
55 Expo
57 Australian animal that munches on eucalyptus leaves
60 Like Lindbergh's famous flight
61 "___ and Let Die" (Paul McCartney hit)

62 Husband of a trophy wife, maybe
64 ___ of March
65 Creme-filled cookie
66 ___ March, Saul Bellow protagonist
67 Future's opposite
68 Gen ___ (thirtysomethings)
69 Poodle or dachshund, e.g.

DOWN

1 Monthly TV bill
2 Separator of continents
3 Margaret Mitchell's Scarlett
4 Serving in Homer Simpson's favorite dinner
5 Boar's mate
6 "At Last" singer James

7 Madeline of "Blazing Saddles"
8 Wabbit's "wival"
9 What a paleontologist reconstructs
10 Pants length measurement
11 Flapper of old toondom
12 Give off
13 Ripped
18 ___ facto
24 Wee one
26 Small dog, in brief
28 Trillion: Prefix
29 Mold's origin
31 First word in many a fairy tale
32 Is a chatterbox
33 Pub draughts
34 One drawn to a flame
35 Loses altitude fast
37 Trade

40 Scandalous 1919 Chicago baseball team
41 Triceratops, e.g.
43 Lifeguard's skill, for short
44 Try to win the hand of
46 Most uncommon
48 Symbol on a flag
50 "___ the One That I Want" ("Grease" song)
52 ___-podge
53 Classics station song
54 Played (with)
55 Freak (out)
56 Opera set in ancient Egypt
58 Follower of new or golden
59 Neighbor of Cambodia
63 Pat gently, as with makeup

by Aimee Lucido, Brown University '13

ACROSS

1 Standing
6 Features of Sophocles plays
10 Peeve, with "off"
14 Rolls for dinner
15 Major constellation?
16 Something an undercover agent might wear
17 In consecutive order
19 Knowing, as a secret
20 Big news on the sports page
21 Bean on the screen
22 Cracker brand
25 Just barely legit
28 Gets used (to)
30 Consideration for when to arrive at the airport: Abbr.
31 But: Lat.
32 It's read from right to left
33 Senseless
35 Give it a go
36 What a slow person may need
39 Nada
42 Word written on the Saudi flag
43 "Dig in!"
47 Summer cooler
48 Place for a ring
49 Astronomer Halley
50 Slip-up
54 Sound accompanying a cloud of smoke
55 It's flashed by an officer
56 Musical set in Buenos Aires
58 Epps of "House"
59 Fragile articles . . . or a hint to the things named by the circled letters
64 Cloud ___
65 Endure
66 Arafat's birthplace
67 Stats for a QB

68 You, to a Quaker
69 Went "tap tap tap" on a keyboard

DOWN

1 What makes a pin spin?
2 Regret
3 Abbr. after a lawyer's name
4 Cheekiness
5 Auditorium balcony, e.g.
6 One-up
7 More arid
8 That, to Tomás
9 "I've got a mule, her name is ___"
10 Pirouette
11 "No, you go, really"
12 Bing Crosby, e.g.
13 Anthony of the Supreme Court
18 Busts

21 Chose from a menu
22 It's smelled when something's fishy
23 Response to "Who wants ice cream?!"
24 Driveway surface
26 ___ by chocolate (calorie-heavy dessert)
27 Explosive Sicilian?
29 "Masterpiece ___"
33 Less active
34 Source of intelligence: Abbr.
37 Sunburn soother
38 Team that has a tankful of rays in the back of its ballpark
39 It's driven over the ice between periods
40 The "King" in "The Last King of Scotland"
41 Locket, often
44 Excessively

45 Game featuring 108 cards
46 Alternative to a print version: Abbr.
49 Christine's lover in "The Phantom of the Opera"
51 Shrek and Fiona, in "Shrek"
52 Witherspoon of "Legally Blonde"
53 Egg-shaped
57 Ambassador's asset
59 Alternative to a Philly cheesesteak
60 Cheerleader's cheer
61 Cup's edge
62 Before, in verse
63 Garden shop offering

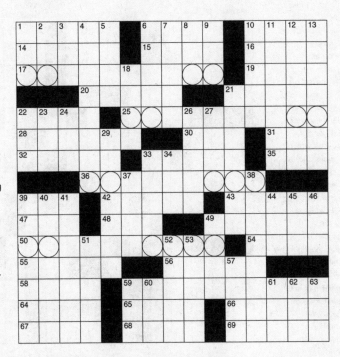

by Eshan Mitra, Brown University '12

ACROSS

1 Org. known for drilling?
5 Masseur's target
9 Soap operas, essentially
14 Offshore
15 What adolescents may fight
16 Bit of dental work
17 Where lead weights grow?
19 Horatio who wrote about down-and-out boys
20 How babies may be carried
21 Bit of a Coleridge poetry line?
23 Takes it easy
26 Nine-digit ID
27 Harvard degree earned by J.F.K. in 1956
30 10 of them make a thou
32 "Take a Chance on Me" group
36 Little battery
37 "Let's call it ___" ("We're even")
38 S O S's, essentially
39 Ammo for idiots?
42 Bert's "Sesame Street" buddy
43 Actress Stewart
44 ___ mater (brain cover)
45 Cheeky chatter
46 Surgical inserts
47 What's up?
48 Gulager of "The Virginian"
50 "Saturday Night Live" segments
52 "Shut up!" . . . or a phonetic hint to this puzzle's theme
56 No-good sort
60 ___ wait
61 Toy house door support?
64 Verdi aria

65 German port
66 ___ Minor
67 "Marat/Sade" playwright Peter
68 Pushing the envelope
69 Singer Perry with the 2010 #1 hit "California Gurls"

DOWN

1 Enthralled
2 Munch Museum's locale
3 German: Abbr.
4 Certain cigarette
5 Capital of Nepal
6 Big name in A.T.M.'s
7 Single
8 Ball supporters
9 Sends cyberjunk
10 Everything considered
11 Lady ___
12 "Lemme ___!"

13 Balkan native
18 Wedding gown fabric
22 Long-eared farm animal
24 Layout
25 Equine areas
27 Works as a stevedore
28 Object of Petrarch's passion
29 Curses
31 Only coach to win both N.F.L. and A.F.L. championships
33 Prompts on answering machines
34 Hand-dyed fabric
35 Analyze
38 Bandage, across the pond
40 Dog treats
41 Not expected
46 Take to court

49 "Peanuts" boy with a blanket
51 Pat of "Wheel of Fortune"
52 Muffed
53 Homeland of Joyce and Yeats
54 Helen Mirren's crowning role, informally?
55 It takes a toll: Abbr.
57 Astronaut's letters
58 Cry during a recess game
59 Web site with a "Buy It Now" option
62 Help
63 Accurate throw

by Zoe Wheeler, Brown University '12

45

ACROSS

1 Plunge
5 More dishonorable
10 "What ___!" ("That was fun!")
14 "I loved, loved, loved that!" review
15 Capital of Ghana
16 Fitzgerald who sang "A-Tisket A-Tasket"
17 "Designing Women" actress is intelligent?
19 Bridle part
20 "Excuse me . . ."
21 Husband-to-be
23 Little pooches
27 Person producing Bordeaux or Beaujolais
28 What a gofer is sent on
29 Takes little steps
30 Jumped
31 Willy with a chocolate factory
32 The Windy City, for short
35 Viva ___
36 Does some mending
37 Pleased
38 Suffix with Siam
39 Daring
40 Roger who played 007
41 Batter's position
43 It might produce a snore in Sonora
44 Capital of Suffolk, England
46 Hold
47 Saying "Please" and "How do you do?," say
48 Tense
49 Chief Norse god
50 "Blondie" cartoonist is not old?
56 Chop up
57 Anouk of le cinéma
58 Mongols' home
59 Fifth Avenue landmark
60 Lords and ladies
61 Retained

DOWN

1 Nickname of a 6'7" former basketball great
2 "Norma ___"
3 Eggs
4 Cross or Parker
5 Clobbered
6 Topmost points
7 Many an e-mail "click here" offer
8 Go astray
9 Squealers
10 Infuse with carbon dioxide
11 "Fatal Attraction" actress is nearby?
12 Girl who went through a looking glass
13 Less addled
18 Superdome player
22 Machu Picchu resident
23 Look (into)
24 Cookies in a box lunch
25 "White Rabbit" singer is smooth?
26 Open the mouth wide
27 "My cousin" in a 1992 film
29 Man with a code
31 Keep an eye on
33 Mates for does
34 Notions
36 Corner sitter's headwear
37 "Anything ___"
39 Trot or canter
40 Like eyes when you're getting nostalgic, maybe
42 Twists and turns, as a tendril
43 Drunkards
44 Products for music downloads
45 Speakers' places
46 Nervous person in a hospital waiting room, perhaps
48 Use a stop clock on
51 Hurry
52 "Mighty" fine home for a squirrel?
53 "What's the ___?"
54 Tuck's partner
55 Gangster's gun

by Bernice Gordon

46

ACROSS
1 "The Hobbit" hero
6 College V.I.P.'s
11 Drs.' org.
14 ___ flu
15 Mother ___
16 Defeat by just a tad
17 Entree on many a Chinese menu
20 Pioneering anti-AIDS drug
21 Blackener of Santa's boots
22 Oscar winner Jannings
23 "No shirt, no shoes, no service," e.g.
25 Cramped alternative to a basement
29 Clear the board
31 "I could ___ horse!"
32 Signs to heed
34 Rotting
38 Pastor, for short
39 Pets . . . or what the starts of 17-, 25-, 50- and 61-Across are all kinds of
42 It can be cast
43 Tabriz residents
45 "Goodnight" girl of old song
47 Greek peak
48 Amber is a fossilized one
50 Old New Yorkers, e.g.
54 Lots
57 Prefix with cultural
58 Intl. group with many generals
60 Big milestone for a young co.
61 Basic hotel banquet entree
66 Still
67 Anticipate
68 River that drains more than 20% of France
69 Date
70 Labor's partner
71 Attack

DOWN
1 King of the elephants in a children's book series
2 Trooper on the highway
3 "The Loco-Motion" singer, 1962
4 Dracula's altered form
5 Telephone numbers without letters
6 Prior to
7 Island south of Sicily
8 Suffix with direct
9 Small change: Abbr.
10 It may precede "Don't let anyone hear!"
11 Inner self
12 Make like
13 Beatles record label
18 Fabled fliers
19 Settle a debt with
24 Directional suffix
26 Sports Illustrated span
27 Feature of many a bodice
28 Equilibrium
30 Franciscans' home
32 ". . . ___ quit!"
33 Debussy's "La ___"
34 Affairs
35 Facial recognition aid
36 Diarist Anaïs
37 "___ whiz!"
40 News agency that was the first to report on Sputnik
41 Genetic materials
44 Mobile phone giant
46 Small inlet
48 Shows shock, e.g.
49 Book after Neh.
50 ___ breath
51 Concur
52 Where Minos reigned
53 Out of shape
55 Word with grand or soap
56 Largish musical group
59 Many works at the Met
62 Patsy
63 Eero Saarinen designed its J.F.K. terminal
64 Viking ship need
65 Runner Sebastian

by Adam G. Perl

ACROSS

1 Dweller on an Asian peninsula
6 Ballgoer, for short
9 Steamed
14 Whack-___
15 Org. doing atmospheric tests
16 Meeting point
17 Gifts for divas
18 Shoreline indentation
19 Has only half-servings, maybe
20 *Turn-of-the-millennium explorer
23 Saudi "son of"
24 Punk rocker ___ Vicious
25 Immobile
28 Hounds
30 *1996 Grammy winner for the album "Falling Into You"
34 "Not a chance!"
36 Kind of place to the left of the decimal point
37 1,055 joules: Abbr.
38 *Treaty of Versailles signer
43 "Give ___ little time"
44 Pitcher Maddux who won four straight Cy Young Awards
45 Cleopatra held it close
46 *Point in a planet's orbit that's closest to the sun
50 Attract
53 Expensive violin, for short
54 ___ pad
56 Before, to Byron
57 Subject of a children's song associated with the vowels in the answer to each starred clue
61 Overly thin
64 Fertility clinic samples
65 Put on, as cargo
66 Sleep disorder
67 "___ the ramparts . . ."
68 "Mr. Belvedere" actress Graff
69 Brenda of comics
70 Promgoers: Abbr.
71 Risked

DOWN

1 Catch that might be mounted
2 It multiplies by dividing
3 Becoming discouraged
4 Beth preceder
5 Some survey responses
6 Ridicule
7 Like some battles
8 Sounds heard by 57-Across
9 World's fourth-most populous country
10 Restricted, with "in"
11 Tool used by Hansel and Gretel's father
12 King ___
13 What's extracted from soil to get oil?
21 Singer Ocasek of the Cars
22 Tendon
26 Tool used in thoracic surgery
27 Kansas canine
29 Carrier with a hub in Copenhagen
31 Second in line?
32 Abbr. on a bank statement
33 Carmelite, for one
35 Sanctuary fixture
38 Any singer with Gladys Knight
39 Delivery persons' assignments: Abbr.
40 Judicial title role for Stallone
41 Slippery swimmer
42 It was dropped in the '60s
47 Worker whose job always has a new wrinkle?
48 Hollywood treasures
49 Silent assent
51 Francis of "What's My Line?"
52 Kind of bliss
55 Nonliquid state
58 Sounds heard by 57-Across
59 Maintain
60 "The Lion King" role
61 Nonliquid state
62 Likely
63 Italian article

by Peter A. Collins

ACROSS

1 Name repeated in the lyric "Whatever ___ wants, ___ gets"
5 Teeter-totter
11 ___ Moines
14 Apple computer
15 Hitting of a golf ball
16 Nothing's opposite
17 Shows petulant anger
19 "Fee, ___, foe, fum"
20 Cheri formerly of "S.N.L."
21 Exam for H.S. seniors
22 Seep
23 Gets lucky
27 Hot tar, e.g.
29 "Here ___ comes, Miss America"
30 Heir, but not an heiress
31 ___ mater
33 "Lucky Jim" author Kingsley
36 Painter Picasso
40 Doesn't stonewall, say
43 Pro ___ (perfunctory)
44 Tiny time unit: Abbr.
45 Like an omelet
46 Toronto's prov.
48 ___ Pérignon
50 Lone Star State nickname
51 Reacts slightly
57 Run amok
58 Cheer for a matador
59 "Ave ___" (Latin prayer)
62 Fourth of July celebration inits.
63 Shows affection unexpectedly
66 They, in Marseille
67 Eight English kings

68 Fitzgerald known as the First Lady of Song
69 Volleyball court divider
70 How china may be sold
71 Possible response to a grabby boyfriend

DOWN

1 Quick weight loss option, informally
2 Leave out
3 Recent arrival
4 Ghana's capital
5 Opposite of NNW
6 Co. that oversees the 21-Across
7 Rub out
8 Couches
9 Dogs whose tails curl up the back

10 Rainy
11 Actor Willem
12 Doolittle of "Pygmalion"
13 Streamlined
18 Chart-toppers
22 Highly decorative
24 Addams who created "The Addams Family"
25 Muscular fellow
26 Knocks on the noggin
27 Large iron hook
28 Medley
32 Not quite
34 100 is average for them
35 Soft leather
37 Cause of goose bumps, perhaps
38 Pricey seating section

39 Gem with colored bands
41 Carvey who used to say "Well, isn't that special?"
42 Environmental sci.
47 Gov't securities
49 Papa's partner
51 Boston N.H.L.'er
52 Window or middle alternative
53 Raise a glass to
54 Justice Kagan
55 Senior, junior and sophomore
56 Rice wines
60 Cuba, por ejemplo
61 "Rush!," on an order
63 ___ Na Na
64 Soapmaker's need
65 Fast jet, for short

by Janice M. Putney

49

ACROSS

1 Cornfield sounds
5 Scarf material
9 Any member of the genus Homo
14 "___ happens . . ."
15 Black
16 In ___ (not yet born)
17 Prevalent
18 Having two or three kids in a family, nowadays
19 What to "Come see the softer side of," in a slogan
20 Two charts?
23 ___ v. Wade
24 Nav. rank
25 Severely affected
27 Dr. Seuss title
32 Gloom's partner
33 Shipment to a smeltery
34 Audited a class, say
36 Winter highway department needs
39 See 43-Across
41 Like some stock
43 With 39-Across, kind of engine
44 Massage
46 Retro photo tone
48 New Orleans-to-Detroit dir.
49 Some airport data: Abbr.
51 Drained
53 Danced at Rio's Carnival, maybe
56 Homer Simpson's Indian friend
57 Mideast grp.
58 Edit?
64 Sharp
66 Recipe step starter
67 Approve
68 Implement for an apple
69 Israel's Golda
70 "Lonesome" tree
71 Lets (up)
72 Basic subj. for a surgeon
73 Goals

DOWN

1 Fault-find
2 Large part of a world atlas
3 Coffee shop convenience for a laptop
4 Not mono
5 Bird spec
6 ___ about (approximately)
7 Gumbo staple
8 ___ node
9 Point on a line?
10 Suffix with suburban
11 A bushel of Boscs?
12 Boo-boo
13 Gave medicine
21 Raggedy ___ (dolls)
22 Concealed
26 Full or half nelson
27 What a debtor might be in
28 Algerian port
29 French father's affairs?
30 Western tribe
31 Spoke (up)
35 Back of the neck
37 Ebb
38 Toboggan, e.g.
40 Cutting remark
42 Shred
45 Fabric dealers, to Brits
47 Coleridge's sacred river
50 Large quantity
52 One side of "the pond"
53 Gap
54 Foil-making giant
55 Comedy alternative
59 Fall place
60 1998 Sarah McLachlan song
61 Related
62 Hourglass fill
63 Prominent features of a "Cats" poster
65 Plumbing fitting

by Michael Torch

ACROSS

1 Supply with more ammo, say
6 Term of endearment
10 Bits of land in la Seine
14 2003 Sandler/ Nicholson comedy
17 1940 Crosby/ Lamour/Hope film that was the first of a "travel" series
18 Yalies
19 Part of NATO: Abbr.
20 "Mad Men" extras
21 Conducted
22 Actor Bert
24 Mystery writer Deighton
25 It may make a ewe turn
27 Big name in baseball cards
30 Starters
33 Gelatinous ingredient in desserts
34 First X or O, say
37 1971 film that was Cybill Shepherd's debut, with "The"
41 1954 Elia Kazan Oscar winner
42 Bout stopper
43 Author Philip
44 Some razors
45 Ergo
46 Pugilists' grp.
47 Blood-typing syst.
49 Mystery writer Edward D. ___
51 Ode title starter
54 World Cup chant
57 Singer/actress Zadora
58 Lomond, e.g.
59 2008 film derived from Dr. Seuss
62 1986 film for which Paul Newman won his only Oscar
63 Inauguration Day highlight
64 Proverbial heptad
65 Addicts

DOWN

1 Less well done
2 ___ Gay, historic plane displayed by the Smithsonian
3 "Encore!"
4 N.L. Central team
5 "I pity the fool" speaker
6 Mideast city whose name, coincidentally, is an anagram of ARABS
7 1935 Marx Brothers romp
8 Proscribe
9 Drivers (on)
10 Drives
11 Sierra ___
12 Bankrupt company in 2001–02 news
13 Fr. holy women
15 Lettuce or kale
16 Corrode
23 Ne'er-do-well
25 Setting for candlelit romance
26 Current unit
28 Henry VIII's sixth
29 Like some suburban homes
30 Scads
31 Go south
32 "___ perpetua" (Idaho's motto)
34 Thursday's eponym
35 College in New Rochelle, N.Y.
36 100-lb. units
38 Triumphant cry
39 Fisherman's 10-pounder, e.g.
40 Mex. miss
45 The sauce
46 Fisherman's spot
47 Lei-person's greeting?
48 Covering for la tête
50 Pietro's ta-tas
51 Olde ___ (historic area, quaintly)
52 Orangish shade
53 Shipboard cries
54 "___ be in England . . ."
55 Old card game with forfeits
56 Photo blowups: Abbr.
58 Vientiane's country
60 Implement in a Millet painting
61 Dallas sch.

by Charles Gersch

ACROSS

1 Frame job
6 Taste
11 Somme summer
14 Love to pieces
15 Clara Barton, e.g.
16 Rank above maj.
17 Michelle Obama and Laura Bush
19 Singer Yoko
20 Sicilian spewer
21 On a grand scale
22 Somersault
23 Highway troopers
26 Of greatest age
29 Poi source
30 The Beach Boys' "___ John B"
31 Drinker's next-day woe
35 Submarine sandwich
36 Early synthesizers
38 Great review
39 Eave
41 Tendon
42 Cubes in a casino
43 E-mail predecessor
45 Oppressive regime
49 ___ Canal, waterway through Schenectady
50 "___ la Douce"
51 Lane of the Daily Planet
55 Beachgoer's shade
56 Tenet of chivalry
59 Had something
60 Assists at a heist
61 Cosmetician Lauder
62 Plural of "la" and "le"
63 West Pointer
64 Unexpected win

DOWN

1 Opposite of "out" in baseball
2 Tighten the writin'?
3 Ripped
4 ___ Major
5 Hamster, for one
6 Speak sharply to
7 Bad news for a taxpayer
8 Sticker
9 Sugar suffix
10 Hi-___ monitor
11 Food-poisoning bacteria
12 Gin's partner
13 Run off to a judge in Vegas, say
18 Allows
22 Put the pedal to the metal
23 Mo. when fall starts
24 Lousy reviews
25 U.R.L. ending that's not "com" or "gov"
26 Mt. McKinley's is 20,320 ft.
27 Oral history
28 Like a dire situation
30 HBO rival
31 Animal in a sty
32 It shows which way the wind blows
33 At any time
34 FF's opposite
36 Spray used on rioters
37 Completely biased
40 Drunk's outburst
41 Jeanne d'Arc, e.g.: Abbr.
43 Least plausible, as an excuse
44 Hellenic H's
45 Daisy part
46 Pontificate
47 Actors speak them
48 Hackneyed
51 Daffy Duck has one
52 Table scraps
53 "Now you're making sense"
54 Proofreader's "reinstate" mark
56 Fond du ___, Wis.
57 Atty.'s org.
58 Fire: Fr.

by Adam G. Perl

ACROSS

1 Andean land
5 Race for hot rods
9 Open, as a pill bottle
14 Photoshop option
15 Actress Skye
16 Indira Gandhi's family name
17 *Bid adieu, informally
19 Live
20 Family beginnings
21 Boise-to-Phoenix dir.
23 Thanksgiving invitee, commonly: Abbr.
24 Is on the hunt
26 *Failure by a narrow margin
28 Captain's record
29 Gorilla famously taught to use sign language
31 "Brain" of a computer, briefly
32 Topographic map notation: Abbr.
34 Lavish affection (on)
36 Beasts of burden
40 *Like Oprah Winfrey and Michael Jordan
43 Villa ___
44 Take ___ of (sample)
45 Where a pear's seeds are
46 Spot for a shot
48 Not a major haircut
50 Flamenco cry
51 *It's often ordered à la mode
55 Meddle (with)
57 'Do that one would rarely wear a hat with
58 Online portal since Windows 95 was launched
59 Book of divine guidance
60 Argot
62 Singer of the lyric formed by the ends of the answers to the four starred clues
66 Building wing, e.g.

67 French brainchild
68 It may be off the wall
69 Irritable
70 Fruity drinks
71 Card game popular in Germany

DOWN

1 Mac alternatives
2 Never-ratified women-related measure, for short
3 King of the Cowboys
4 Violinist's stroke
5 Coca-Cola Zero, e.g.
6 Rips off
7 "___ better?"
8 Fliers in V's
9 Like a good golf score
10 Novel
11 Dear, in 12-Down
12 Van Gogh locale
13 Attracts

18 Fatty part of an egg
22 ___ fly (certain baseball hit, for short)
24 Answer, in court
25 Husband of Pocahontas
26 Characteristic of bland food and bad dressers
27 Swing or rock
30 Coffee cultivated on Mauna Loa
33 Life-or-death
35 Mideast noble
37 Cleavage-revealing dress feature
38 Hall-of-Famer Combs who played with Gehrig and Ruth
39 Malfoy's look, in the Harry Potter books
41 The Changing of the Guard, e.g.
42 Abstracts

47 Brit. legislators
49 Painter Chagall
51 Chopin's "Polonaise in ___ Major, Op. 53"
52 Group of lions
53 Places for ornamental fish
54 Neighbor of Bhutan
56 No enrollees at Smith College
59 Joint for a beggar?
61 Caught
63 Bizarre
64 "I caught you!"
65 Word after waste and want

by Paula Gamache

ACROSS

1 Red October detector
6 Mystified
11 Support grp. for the troops
14 Pong maker
15 Hardly chic
16 Black goo
17 1970 James Taylor hit
19 Egg cells
20 See 2-Down
21 Go over
22 Mischievous rural pastime
25 Kind of agent
30 "I can ___"
31 Hatch on the Senate floor
32 Start of a dog owner's sign
35 Keeping your elbows off the table, e.g.
40 Surrounded by
41 Basslike fish
42 Complaints, informally
45 Renter
46 Classic Dana Carvey character, with "the"
50 Eastern discipline
51 Bygone warship
57 1989 play about Capote
58 Sound of capitalism? . . . or a hint to the starts of 17-, 22-, 35- and 46-Across
60 Orders at a restaurant
61 Restaurant order, with "the"
62 Tempt
63 Bus. card info
64 Luxurious
65 Building material in "The Three Little Pigs"

DOWN

1 Bombproof, say
2 Big name in the 20-Across business
3 Undercover buster
4 Turf
5 Iranian money
6 Supplement
7 "Presumed Innocent" author
8 Brainy
9 Prefix with dermis
10 Rand who wrote "Civilization is the process of setting man free from men"
11 Best of all possible worlds
12 Idiot ___
13 "High," in the Homeland Security Advisory System
18 Common crystals, chemically
21 Body organs associated with anger
23 "The Hurt Locker" setting
24 Browse
25 Mail-order option
26 ___ Gold, agent on "Entourage"
27 Samovar
28 Singer honored on a 2008 U.S. postage stamp
29 Lacking brio
32 Flower's home
33 Frequent Weekly World News subjects, briefly
34 Wordplay, e.g.
36 Full of calories
37 How-___
38 Nail holder
39 Just make (out)
42 Swath maker
43 Chest
44 Lordly
45 Boston suburb
47 Capt.'s inferior
48 Ball's partner
49 Valentine embellishment
52 Capt.'s inferiors
53 "Ri-i-ight!"
54 Sweets
55 Designer Schiaparelli
56 Ton
58 "___ Father . . ."
59 Tire abbr.

by Ian Livengood

54

ACROSS

1 Close with a bang
5 Crimson Tide, to fans
9 Loss's opposite
13 Aria da ___
14 Establishment with hair dryers
15 Hip about
16 Muscat is its capital
17 Warning
18 Slightly open, as a door
19 Shifting piece of the earth's crust
22 Exist naturally
23 ___ Royal Highness
24 Cut (off), as with a sweeping motion
27 Supped
28 ___ Vista (search engine)
31 Dwell
33 Extraterrestrial's transportation
35 Lotion ingredient
38 Psychology 101 topic
39 Sail holder
40 Quadrennial soccer championship
45 Traveled with Huck Finn, e.g.
46 Those, in Tijuana
47 ___-Town (Cubbies' home)
50 Surgeons' workplaces, for short
51 Sponsors' spots
53 Showy cock's object of affection
55 Los Angeles Philharmonic summer venue
59 Dud
61 The Hunter constellation
62 Merle Haggard's "___ From Muskogee"
63 "I bet you won't go bungee jumping," e.g.
64 Give 10% to one's church
65 A/C opening
66 Gave the boot
67 Impudence
68 Energy output units

DOWN

1 Nova ___, Canada
2 Bemoan
3 Cochise or Geronimo
4 Del ___ Foods
5 Storied isle near Java
6 Actor Baldwin
7 Undergo transformation, as one image into another
8 Stag's pride
9 Billy or nanny
10 Oscar winner Huston
11 Make ___ habit
12 Neither's partner
14 In a rational way
20 ___ vaccine
21 General location
25 Poems of praise
26 Bouncy
29 Stadium level
30 Viewpoint
32 Drainage pit
33 Impressive act
34 Dwellers on Mount Olympus
35 Hardly a close-cut hairdo
36 Fabricator
37 Not on land, as an oil rig
41 Prosperity
42 Stock in nonstandard quantities
43 Gangster known as Scarface
44 Exploited
47 Snug necklace
48 Felling
49 Small bays
52 Neighbor of Israel
54 Over
56 ___ page (newspaper part)
57 Jokesters
58 Sounds of amazement
59 Prescription safety org.
60 Too permissive

by Robert Fisher

Note: The answers to the 12 starred clues have something in common. What is it? (Answer in Notepad)

ACROSS

1 *Reno and 38-Across, for two
7 Maze runner
13 All piled up
15 *Procter & Gamble deodorizer
16 *Sweet Italian wine
17 *Fitting
18 Indy initials
19 Mauna ___
20 Cheater's utterance
24 Cavalry blade
26 Band with the 2008 song "Electric Feel"
30 "It's all coming back to me now"
32 Parental palindrome
33 *The second "M" of MGM
34 *Roundabout, for one
36 ___ Nevada
37 Downed
38 See 1-Across
40 Bailed-out co. in 2009 news
41 Latter-day Saint
43 *Actress Lewis of "Natural Born Killers"
45 *Hanna-Barbera's ___ Doggie
46 Stewart of "The Daily Show"
47 Knight's need
48 Dead river?
49 Mongoose's foe
51 Small vortex
52 Stop start?
53 Lode deposit
55 *Cosmetics chain whose name comes from the Greek for "beauty"
59 *Nadya Suleman, mother of 14, familiarly
64 *Nays
65 Productive
66 Hannibal of "The Silence of the Lambs"
67 *Remove nails from

DOWN

1 Halpert of "The Office"
2 Santa ___
3 Not wide: Abbr.
4 Canadian query closers
5 Oolong and others
6 Puts (away), as for safekeeping
7 Outcast
8 Start of a spell
9 Dude
10 Workout unit
11 ___ dye
12 Parisian possessive
14 Nickname of the dictator who said "I know the Haitian people because I am the Haitian people"
15 Like some U.F.O. sightings
20 Sleepers
21 Game in which only one team scores
22 Working well together
23 Private eye
25 Heist of a sort
26 Fannie ___
27 Did the watusi, e.g.
28 Deserved
29 "Coriolanus" or "Richard III"
31 Missouri city, informally
33 Some skirts
35 Actor Holm
36 G string?
39 Car option that slides open
42 Mingle
44 Summer on the Seine
46 Pop's ___ Brothers
49 Apple implement
50 Rainbowlike
52 Part of a melody
54 Raison d'___
55 "___ Digital Shorts"
56 Want ad abbr.
57 Common pipe material, briefly
58 Trendy
60 Like some stocks, for short
61 1,000 G's
62 Suffix with pay or plug
63 Cat call

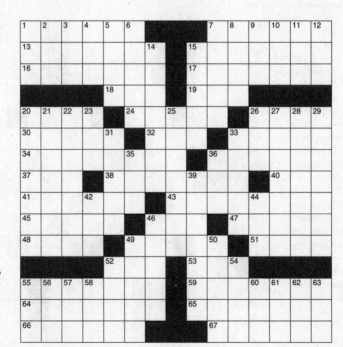

by Jose Chardiet

56

ACROSS

1 "The Da Vinci Code" priory
5 Disgusting-tasting
9 The first to stab Caesar
14 Feminine suffix
15 Key point
16 Gordon and Ginsburg
17 Dog in whodunits
18 Fine-tune
19 Register
20 Place with a "You Are Here" map
23 Brew source
24 Dermal opening?
25 Fleet letters
26 Packed away
28 Left at sea
30 Anchor-hoisting equipment
33 Go straight
35 Howard who parodied Adolf
36 Affirmative actions?
37 Longtime Greenwich Village music venue, with "the"
40 Source of bubbly
43 The other army
44 Innumerable
48 Protection for Pelé
51 Slowly, to Solti
52 Ground breaker
53 Breakfast orders at a 55-Down, briefly
54 Altar agreement
56 Muslim convert in 1964 news
57 Glen Campbell hit, the last word of which is this puzzle's theme
61 Half of diez
62 Verve
63 Instrument played with a mallet
64 "I don't care if they do"
65 Learning by flash cards, e.g.
66 Seek out
67 Decrease, as support
68 Poll closing?
69 Badlands locale: Abbr.

DOWN

1 Five-pointed creature
2 Like most gym rats
3 Keeping up with
4 Tide type
5 TV blocking device
6 Having a twist
7 One getting an inspiration?
8 Will figure
9 Actor Richard of "Rambo" films
10 Unpaid sitter, perhaps
11 Like some dirty windshields
12 "Through the Looking-Glass" laugh
13 Hand communication: Abbr.
21 Lab dish inventor
22 Hold in regard
27 Some R.P.I. grads
29 Batpole user
31 Mideast leader: Var.
32 Core group
34 Japan's highest point: Abbr.
38 Wedding reception participants, often
39 Hose material
40 Smokestack emission
41 More ostentatious
42 Connect with
45 Sulky
46 Emory University's home
47 Hanging in there
49 "Beat it, kid!"
50 Get wider
55 Where hash is "slung"
58 E-mailed a dupe to
59 Jillions
60 Orders at a 55-Down
61 A.L. Central city

by Alan Arbesfeld

ACROSS

1 Officials behind batters
5 Scarlett whose final film words are "I'll never be hungry again"
10 Dame Hess at a piano
14 What to call a king
15 Caution light's color
16 Chick's chirp
17 Preowned
18 Where Jodie lives?
20 Survey a second time
22 ___ de cologne
23 To the ___ (fully)
24 With 53-Across, where Victoria lives?
28 Say "Boo!" to, say
30 Ernie on the links
31 Moonshine device
32 Dirty dishes often collect in them
33 Hair colorers
35 Weekly TV show with guest hosts, for short
36 Broadcast
37 Where Donna lives?
41 A clown might get it in the face
42 Jr.'s son
43 Heady brews
46 Current conductors
49 Rachel Maddow's network
51 Singleton
52 Nonreactive, chemically
53 See 24-Across
55 Co. with a lot of connections?
56 Inexact no.
58 Multigenerational stories
59 Where Sally lives?
64 Starchy tropical root
65 Not working
66 Camel caravan's stop
67 "You too?" à la Caesar
68 Trial run
69 Scents
70 Well-kept

DOWN

1 Seized, as the throne
2 Scroogelike
3 Debaters' basic assumptions
4 Many a family car
5 Clodhopper
6 Payer of some hosp. bills
7 "Washboard" muscles
8 Give a new version of, as a story
9 Square footage
10 Dashboard abbr.
11 Royal attendant in a Gilbert and Sullivan operetta
12 Comment
13 Uppermost points
19 Moscow's land
21 Dell or Toshiba products, for short
25 "Who's there?" response
26 "Knotty" wood
27 Cry from a bailiff when a judge walks in
29 Around, in a date
34 "Fantastic!"
36 Cover story
38 Covered with a fine spray
39 Bowlers' targets
40 Stretch
44 Former Web reference from Microsoft
45 Ushers to the exit
46 Nintendo product for the gym-averse, maybe
47 Not outdoors
48 Disgusts
49 Wild-riding squire of "The Wind in the Willows"
50 Savings acct. alternatives
54 Consumed
57 "Scram!"
60 Permit
61 Troops' support grp.
62 Walter Raleigh or Walter Scott
63 Twisty road curve

by Lynn Lempel

58

ACROSS

1 Mynah bird, e.g.
6 Has to
10 Send by FedEx or UPS
14 Mrs. Perón
15 Worker welfare grp.
16 Noted tower site
17 Seventh day, in the Bible?
19 Westernmost Aleutian
20 "I'll have another"
21 "Tired blood" tonic
23 Cheesy sandwich
25 Having all one's marbles
26 Truth stretcher
30 Go hog wild
32 P, in Greece
35 One way to think or read
36 Homo vis-à-vis humans
37 Homo sapiens
38 "The Wizard of Oz" coward
39 What a roof is usually built on
40 Dagger
41 Bit of Web video gear
42 Small earrings
43 A sheriff may round one up
44 Horatian creation
45 Hunter's garb, for short
46 Like a mud puddle
47 Cheer (for)
49 Vintners' valley
51 Cash-back deals
54 Condiment at Nathan's
59 Touch on
60 $10 bill enclosed in a Valentine card?
62 "Jeepers!"
63 Pioneering D.J. Freed
64 Home, sweet home
65 Picnic intruders
66 Join with a blowtorch
67 Religious council

DOWN

1 Note from the boss
2 "Terrible" czar
3 What a D.J. speaks into
4 Tabloids twosome
5 Ricocheted, as a cue ball
6 Tasty mushroom
7 Be hooked on
8 Thick carpet
9 Brings on a date
10 Onetime colonial power in the Philippines
11 One-third of a strikeout?
12 "That's all there ___ it!"
13 Left-handed Beatle
18 Term of address used by Uncle Remus
22 Slum vermin
24 Trample underfoot
26 Edie of "The Sopranos"
27 Homeric epic
28 Statue of a post-W.W. II baby?
29 Sloppy joe holder
31 Bed-and-breakfasts
33 Unduly severe
34 Like a good singer
36 Wearing a long face
39 Result of a governor's signing
40 "Inka Dinka ___"
42 Loch Lomond local
43 Blood bank supplies
46 Cowboy boot feature
48 Solemn vows
50 Make changes in
51 Sitar music
52 Black, to bards
53 Dover ___
55 Man-shaped mug
56 In a bit, in poems
57 Give a makeover
58 Did some batiking
61 Kilmer of film

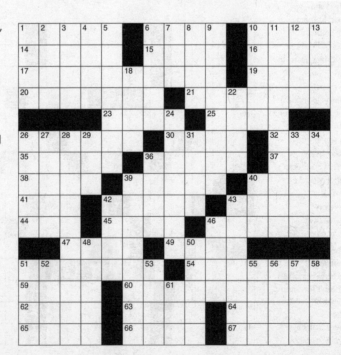

by Fred Piscop

ACROSS

1 City SSW of Jacksonville
6 Physics units
10 First of two before-and-after pictures
14 Mannerly
15 Stir (up)
16 "No prob"
17 *Megadeth's music genre
19 "Now!"
20 European tongue
21 Cornerstone abbr.
22 Green bug
23 Increase in increments, with "up"
25 Sign in the bleachers
27 *"The Lion King" song
31 Enlightened Buddhist
34 ___ the beginning
35 Neighbor of Hung.
36 You may take one before dinner
37 Swedish-based international clothing giant . . . or a hint to the answers to the six starred clues
39 Dr. Johnny Fever's station, in 1970s–'80s TV
40 Hi-tech heart
41 Spanish bath
42 Kind of buddy
43 *Hilton head, e.g.
47 One of the three original Muses
48 Knocked someone out, say
52 Viking training camp?
54 "The Godfather" composer Nino
56 "I finished"
57 Who once remarked "You can't stay mad at somebody who makes you laugh"
58 *The Father of American Public Education
60 Extra: Abbr.
61 German word slangily used to mean "extremely"
62 Circle measures
63 Germany's ___ Canal
64 Internet ___ (viral phenomenon)
65 English race site

DOWN

1 Autumn hue
2 Old Olds
3 "Stop, matey!"
4 Real-time online conversation
5 Prince ___ Khan
6 1974 Mocedades hit
7 Film director Martin
8 Politician's greeting
9 Partner of poivre, in French seasoning
10 It's "short and stout" in a children's song
11 *Lines on a football field
12 Morales who played a 13-Down officer on TV
13 See 12-Down
18 Docile
22 Part of a Latin 101 trio
24 Symbol of a position
26 Shiite leader
28 Sheer fabric
29 One seeing red?
30 Like 12-hour clocks
31 "The Nazarene" author Sholem
32 "___ Man"
33 *Society
37 2004 Olympics gymnastics star Paul or Morgan
38 Organism that doesn't require oxygen
39 Colorful almanac feature
41 Ran
42 Busy type
44 Sign up
45 Rubbernecking
46 Auto financing co.
49 A lot
50 Film composer Morricone
51 Material in a "Canadian tuxedo"
52 Criticism
53 Lightsaber wielder
55 Utah city
58 What fans do
59 Poetic preposition

by Finn Vigeland

ACROSS

1 Healing ointment
5 Partner
9 David who sang "Space Oddity"
14 1-Across ingredient
15 Enthusiastic
16 Like some on-the-spot wireless networks
17 *Toy that's thrown
19 Point of no return?
20 What an E may stand for
21 Deck wood
23 China's ___ Zedong
24 Like a clear night sky
26 Tic
28 1492, 1776, 2001, etc.
30 Seek divine help from
33 Indent key
36 Back of the neck
38 Silents star Normand
39 Has an exciting opening number, say . . . or what the answer to each starred clue does?
43 Knight's attire
44 Actor Jared
45 Fig. on a vitamin bottle
46 Possible result of an animal bite
48 Door fastener
51 Jimmy of the Daily Planet
53 Bizarre
57 Angsty music genre
59 Look searchingly
61 "Certainly, madame!"
62 Domino's offering
64 *Situation set to explode
66 "Pirates of the Caribbean" locales
67 In the thick of
68 One who ran away with the spoon, in a nursery rhyme
69 Directors Ethan and Joel
70 Slothful
71 Kiln for hops

DOWN

1 Toyland visitors
2 Overhead
3 Bath sponge
4 Dalí's "The Persistence of ___"
5 Invaders in an H. G. Wells story
6 Gardner of film
7 Windshield glare reducer
8 A hexagon has six of them
9 Comeuppance for evil actions, supposedly
10 Laudatory poem
11 *Guitar accessory that adds vibrato
12 Itsy-bitsy bit
13 Canyon sound effect
18 Gardner of mystery
22 Download for an iPhone
25 Fish with a net
27 Sad-sounding car company?
29 Sales pitch
31 Be inclined (to)
32 ___ Korbut, 1972 Soviet gymnastics star
33 Old Russian autocrat
34 Gillette razor
35 *Hoodwink
37 Singers James and Jones
40 Agitate
41 Ignore a property owner's signs, perhaps
42 Warm bedtime beverage
47 Visualize
49 Rock's Mötley ___
50 Bob or beehive
52 Country with Sherpas
54 Finnish cell phone giant
55 "___ who?!"
56 Number in an octet
57 "Ben-Hur," for one
58 Soup with sushi
60 Italia's capital
63 Buddhist sect
65 Brainiac

by Jonah Kagan

ACROSS

1 With 17-Across, event of 10/30/10
6 With 10-Across, sobriquet for Bill O'Reilly used by 39-Across
10 See 6-Across
14 Duck, as a question
15 Real comedian
16 Tolstoy's Karenina
17 See 1-Across
20 Knights
21 White House fiscal grp.
22 Deals in a fantasy league
23 Fashionably old
25 Reuniongoer
27 Buffoon
28 Gambler's best friend?
33 Wizards' and Celtics' org.
36 Winner when heads loses
38 Pi r squared, for a circle
39 Organizer of the 54-/65-Across
41 Organizer of the 1-/17-Across
44 Uffizi display
45 Tempest
47 Troubadour's song
48 Object of loathing
51 Envoy's bldg.
53 "Shake ___!"
54 With 65-Across, event of 10/30/10
57 Song part
61 Duo
63 Breakfast place that's often open 24 hrs.
65 See 54-Across
68 "Caro nome," e.g.
69 Cook in a way, as tuna or beef tenderloin
70 Rehem, say
71 Not straight
72 Award won for 39- and 41-Across's programs
73 "The Fountainhead" hero

DOWN

1 "Darn it!"
2 To have, to Henri
3 Peter of "Casablanca"
4 Deceives
5 They are 3 ft. long
6 Annual coronation site
7 Complete miss in basketball
8 "The Tell-Tale Heart" writer
9 Offered for breeding
10 Eric who played the Hulk in 2003
11 An OK city
12 Throw in a few chips, say
13 Tampa Bay team
18 How a practical joke or a subway train may be taken
19 "Be All You Can Be" group
24 2.5%/year interest, e.g.
26 Rodeo rope
29 Supreme Court's sphere
30 ___ Mountains, Europe/Asia separator
31 Michael of "Scott Pilgrim vs. the World"
32 1918 song girl whose name was sung with a stutter
33 Final Four inits.
34 Brought into the world
35 Utah ski resort
37 Informal reply to "Who's there?"
40 Wager
42 2 or 3 on the Richter scale, maybe
43 Jane Austen meddler
46 Wrestling duo
49 Smog, e.g.
50 Go by, as time
52 S.O.S alternative
55 Tony-winning Rivera
56 Act like an overly protective parent
57 Pierce
58 Ripped
59 Comparable (to)
60 Tidy
62 Cautious
64 Employee discount, e.g.
66 Opposite of masc.
67 Swiss river

by Chris Handman

62

ACROSS

1 Director Lee
4 Big name in sport shirts
8 Dispute
14 Little dipper?
15 Film style
16 Makes less than a killing
17 Cholesterol abbr.
18 Nut with caffeine
19 Grand grounds
20 Comment on life by 52-Across?
23 Like some straw
24 Hangs around
28 Deposit and withdrawal site for 52-Across?
32 Lamebrained
33 Musical Reed
34 Displaying more violence
35 Result of an encounter with 52-Across?
40 Seize for ransom
41 Capek play
42 Mole, e.g.
43 Crib plaything for a young 52-Across?
49 Buffy the Vampire Slayer, e.g.
51 Stiffness
52 See 20-, 28-, 35- and 43-Across
56 Vampire story, e.g.
59 Deuce follower
60 Frozen water, to Wilhelm
61 Hebrew name for God
62 Part of a vampire
63 ___-Foy, Que.
64 Pied Piper's sound
65 Nipper
66 Down

DOWN

1 Like the heart during a horror movie
2 "Sorry, Charlie"
3 Frozen treat
4 Way to pay someone back
5 ___-suiter
6 Like mechanics' hands
7 Void of any va-va-voom
8 Poem title start
9 Ill-fated ship of film
10 Spot to pick up Spot
11 Spanish she-bear
12 Bar fixture, maybe
13 Squeeze (out)
21 Fierce sort, astrologically
22 Sort
25 Awesome, in slang
26 Stink
27 Neighbor of Turk.
29 Tiny bump on a graph
30 ___ Center (Chicago skyscraper)
31 Commercial lead-in to Sweet
34 "Cootie"
35 Carpet feature
36 Month before Nisan
37 Having clean hands
38 Like some parks
39 QB's utterance
40 Speed meas. in Europe
43 Big ___
44 Popsicle choice
45 Pen with a cap
46 "Um . . . O.K."
47 1955 novel that was made into 1962 and 1997 films
48 Obliterated
50 Racy film
53 1920s chief justice
54 Subject of the book "Six Armies in Normandy"
55 N.H.L. venue
56 No. on a map
57 Tokyo, once
58 Melted chocolate, e.g.

by Jay Kaskel

ACROSS

1 Not reacting to pain, say
6 Playboy centerfold, e.g.
11 Col. Sanders's restaurant
14 Go round and round
15 Tennis champ Agassi
16 ". . . ___ he drove out of sight"
17 Aid for a person with a limp
19 Yang's counterpart
20 Sound from a mouse
21 Blue Ribbon beer brewer
23 Brussels ___
26 Arabian V.I.P.'s
27 River past Westminster Palace
28 Party handouts
30 "That's ___!" ("Not true!")
31 Cosmetician Adrien
32 Machine tooth
35 ___ Alamos, N.M.
36 Drug from Colombia
38 "Long ___ and far away . . ."
39 Virgil's 61
40 Long-armed ape, for short
41 Late West Virginia senator Robert
42 W.W. II admiral Chester
44 Island where many a 40-Across lives
46 Disheveled
48 Most boneheaded
49 One out of prison
50 Mick Jagger and bandmates, informally
52 ___ carte
53 1941 Orson Welles classic
58 Architect I. M. ___
59 French word before cuisine or couture
60 Respected tribe member
61 ID on an I.R.S. form
62 ___ a positive note
63 Actress Winona

DOWN

1 Opposite NNE
2 Old "Up, up and away" carrier
3 Texaco's business
4 Irritating
5 In-group
6 Senate gofers
7 Early Peruvian
8 Fargo's home: Abbr.
9 Keats's "Ode on a Grecian ___"
10 Hotel room door feature
11 Nixon's Florida home
12 Pat down, as for weapons
13 Number after a decimal in a price
18 Items in a Planters can
22 ___ Lingus
23 Play for time
24 Showy flowers
25 Creating a ruckus
26 Stereotypical Swedish man's name
28 Writer Kafka
29 Fat as ___
31 Nervous as ___
33 Fairy tale monsters
34 Whom Vladimir and Estragon were waiting for, in a Beckett play
36 War chief Black Horse's tribe
37 Copier input: Abbr.
41 In a quick and lively manner
43 Judge in the O. J. Simpson trial
44 Common shape for a dog biscuit
45 First game of the season
46 Harvests
47 Connections for car wheels
48 Egg carton count
50 Poker variety
51 Latin jazz great Puente
54 Author Fleming or McEwan
55 Put two and two together
56 Jacqueline Kennedy ___ Bouvier
57 Blunder

by Holden Baker

ACROSS

1 Toy gun shot
4 Machine that was often cloned
9 Molecular matter
13 "Don't Bring Me Down" band, for short
14 It may be "golden" in mathematics
15 Kind of shark
16 Where a cowpuncher may work
18 Sweat spot
19 School attended by James Bond . . . and Ian Fleming
20 Big bears
22 Drink made with vodka, coffee liqueur and cream
26 Equipment for Olympian Lindsey Vonn
27 Aunts, in Arles
30 "Exodus" hero
33 Grades in the mid-70s
35 "Arrivederci"
36 "Sorry if that rude word offended you"
40 Double-reed woodwind
41 Prefix with -morphism
42 "What a pleasant surprise!"
43 Letter-writing prisoner, perhaps
46 Quatre+un
48 Play whence the phrase "the most unkindest cut of all"
53 Group for young people coping with parental substance abuse
55 "Othello" villain
56 Green fruit
57 What the last words in 16-, 22-, 36- and 48-Across are
61 ___ fixe

62 "Fiddler on the Roof" milkman
63 Game cube
64 Signs of approval
65 Pictures that may be difficult to focus on
66 Word repeated in a classic "When Harry Met Sally . . ." scene

DOWN

1 Moisten, as grass
2 Animator Don
3 "Same here"
4 Like the verb "to be": Abbr.
5 Sheep's cry
6 Everest, e.g.: Abbr.
7 Selects
8 Any regular on "The View," e.g.
9 Atmosphere, as at a restaurant
10 Quentin who directed "Inglourious Basterds"
11 "I get it already!"
12 Does some lawn work
17 Sinusitis docs
21 1/7 of a Spanish week
23 Kitchen utensil brand name
24 Nothing, in Paris
25 1972 #2 hit for Bill Withers
28 Individually
29 Greenwich Village neighbor
30 Individually
31 "Streamers" playwright David
32 Exhibiting fierce determination
34 Matches, as two tapes
37 Sheriffs' sidekicks

38 Bank guarantor, for short
39 "Five Women" author Jaffe
44 Word that can follow pale, brown or cask
45 Told fibs
47 British monarch beginning in '52
49 Overseas diplomat in N.Y.C., say
50 Little Orphan Annie's dog
51 Texas A&M athlete
52 Rock's Guns N' ___
53 Like, with "to"
54 Beach resort at the entrance to the Lagoon of Venice
58 Model Herzigova
59 Six-Day War land: Abbr.
60 Word with the longest entry in the O.E.D.

by Brendan Emmett Quigley

65

ACROSS

1 The two together
5 In fighting trim
8 Sparks's state
14 Quick as a wink
16 For all, as a restroom
17 Online university staff?
18 Trig function
19 Anthem contraction
20 Phone no.
22 Body designs, informally
23 What Nashville sunbathers acquire?
27 One to hang with
28 Special attention, for short
29 Golf ball's position
30 "Not on ___!"
32 Hasty escape
34 Ballplayer with a 40-Down logo
39 Sign prohibiting sunshades?
43 At attention
44 Sgt. or cpl.
45 Like many fast-food orders
46 Bailed-out insurance co.
49 Local govt. unit
51 Make public
52 Salon jobs from apprentice stylists?
57 Zinging remark
58 Coffee, slangily
59 Nest egg letters
60 Where to find a piece of Turkey
62 "Stop that!" . . . and a hint to the answers to 17-, 23-, 39- and 52-Across
67 Chips away at
68 Seinfeld's eccentric relative
69 Many a Little League rooter
70 "Go team!"
71 Sunbathers catch them

DOWN

1 Coal holder
2 Indivisible
3 Demolitionist's aid
4 Biker's invitation to a friend
5 Former Big Apple mayor La Guardia
6 Global currency org.
7 Lab jobs
8 Atomic centers
9 Brian of ambient music
10 Scenic view
11 Like most Turks
12 Body shop jobs
13 Graph lines
15 1545–63 council site
21 Moray, e.g.
23 Drum accompanying a fife
24 École attendee
25 Emotionally damage
26 Blue-green hue
27 Plexiglas piece
31 Muscle spasm
33 AOL alternative
35 W. C. Fields persona
36 Bar closing time, perhaps
37 Philbin of live TV
38 "P.U.!" inducer
40 See 34-Across
41 "Hamlet" has five
42 Fastball in the dirt, say
47 Kiddingly
48 Prefix with thermal
50 Jeopardy
52 Michelle's predecessor as first lady
53 Goof
54 "Humble" home
55 Come back
56 Zagat, to restaurants
57 Microwave sound
61 Porker's pad
63 Old-time actress Merkel
64 Suffix with pay or plug
65 Driver's one-eighty
66 How-___ (handy books)

by Tracy Gray

ACROSS

1 With 66-Across, subject of this puzzle, born 12/1/1935
6 "Maude" star Arthur
9 With 64-Across, 1-/66-Across movie of 2005
14 "If memory serves . . ."
16 Dress in the Forum
17 . . . of 1987
18 Some tomatoes
19 Faux pas
21 Winter hrs. in St. Louis
22 . . . of 1990
26 __ exchange
27 It's high on the pH scale
28 Silents actor Novarro
29 . . . of 1979
31 Asian nurse
32 Dorothy's state: Abbr.
33 "Too bad!"
34 . . . of 1971
36 . . . of 1973
40 Be up
41 Mayo is in it
42 __ land
43 . . . of 1977
47 Par __
48 Part of l'été
49 A mean Amin
50 . . . of 1983
51 Nelson Mandela's org.
52 Shaded passageway
55 Verdi's very
57 . . . of 1978
62 Close, in verse
63 Feverishness
64 See 9-Across
65 Raiders make them, informally
66 See 1-Across

DOWN

1 Something played out in a theater
2 Spanish she-bear
3 Geometric suffix
4 Demoisturized, in commercial names
5 Palace workers
6 Flock sounds
7 Heavenly
8 Hall-of-Famer Walter who was a Dodger manager for 23 years
9 No. on a car
10 __ Z
11 Male with whiskers
12 Top-level
13 Get a move on
15 Early fifth-century year
20 Surround with a glow
22 Sheik's mount
23 Spiritual guide
24 One-named 1970s–'80s supermodel
25 Live together
27 Vitamin involved in cell metabolism
29 "Keep them coming, Juan!"
30 Amazement
32 TV's __ Lee
35 Scot's not
36 Show announced by Don Pardo for 30+ years, for short
37 Construction worker's lunch container
38 H. G. Wells people
39 Phoned
41 Neatened, in a way
43 Certain travel guide
44 "Stop! You've got it all wrong!"
45 Centers
46 Unmoored
47 Hank with voices on "The Simpsons"
52 Left side
53 Places where the Daily Racing Form is read, in brief
54 Celtic sea god
56 Get bronze
58 Excellent, slangily
59 Lube (up)
60 Way: Abbr.
61 Dict. listing

by Caleb Madison

ACROSS

1 Native Louisianan
6 Sass
9 Future's opposite
13 Make a grand speech
14 Physician's org.
15 Pinnacles
17 Appreciated
18 In good order
20 Adam and Eve's first home
21 Watch intently
22 Actor Stephen of "Michael Collins"
23 Annie Oakley, for one
26 Bandleader Shaw and others
29 Mate for 60-Down
30 Combat stress syndrome
35 Watch chains
38 Disney frame
39 Last installment of "The Godfather"
41 Cultural support org.
42 "Stop right there!"
44 Pull a bed prank on
46 Cow sound
48 Funnywoman Boosler
49 Wool gatherer
55 Thanksgiving side dish
56 Rosebush hazards
57 Make woozy
61 Bootblack's service
63 "The Taming of the ___"
64 Ankle bones
65 Title for Galahad
66 "___ bleu!"
67 Viewed
68 Tetley product
69 Set of cultural values

DOWN

1 Porter who wrote "Night and Day"
2 Saharan
3 Gyllenhaal of "Love & Other Drugs"
4 Knife, fork or spoon
5 Rorem who composed the opera "Our Town"
6 Modern surgical tool
7 Zoot-suiter's "Got it!"
8 Noah's ark groupings
9 Congregation leader
10 German exclamation
11 Wagers from those in the know
12 Shelter made of buffalo skin, maybe
16 Blacken, as a steak
19 Oom-___
21 Succeed in appearing to be
24 Lend a hand
25 Buffoon
26 Yiddish writer Sholem
27 Perlman of "Cheers"
28 "Go on . . ."
31 Prince's title: Abbr.
32 Plains Indian
33 Round fig.
34 Writers of bad checks
36 Has-___
37 Overfill
40 ___ of Wight
43 One on the Statue of Liberty is almost three feet long
45 Construction worker
47 Chooses to participate
49 The "S" in CBS: Abbr.
50 Laughs
51 Library admonition
52 Lift
53 W.W. II correspondent Pyle
54 "It's the end of ___"
58 St. Louis's Gateway ___
59 O
60 Mates for a 29-Across
62 Language suffix
63 Opposite of NNW

by Richard Chisholm

68

ACROSS

1 Neighbor of Kuwait
5 Sugar source
10 Ice Follies venue
14 Half of Mork's sign-off
15 Volunteer's cry
16 Arabian Peninsula sultanate
17 Governor in Austin?
19 Area that may have stained-glass windows
20 Come together
21 Card player's boo-boo
23 All the world's one, to the Bard
25 Unwelcome result of a shopping spree?
27 Chow down
28 Give kudos
30 "Black gold"
31 Sluggers' stats
33 Life stories, for short
35 Nut jobs
39 Bit of Sunday TV scheduling . . . or a hint to 17-, 25-, 50- and 59-Across
42 Aid in finding sunken ships
43 Part of a wedding cake
44 Jackson or Winslet
45 Sock hop locale
47 Galifianakis of "The Hangover"
49 Actress Farrow
50 Airport baggage handler?
54 Like half of a pair of dentures
56 Do the work of a florist or an orchestrator
57 "S O S," e.g.
58 Belly laugh
59 Sheep's accuser?
64 Cut and paste, say
65 Pungent-smelling
66 Lowdown
67 Say isn't so
68 Presidents Tyler and Taylor, for two
69 Plastic brick brand

DOWN

1 Abbr. at the end of a co. name
2 Cheerleader's cry
3 Walt Disney's specialty
4 "The Caine Mutiny" captain
5 Oven user's aid
6 Leave dumbstruck
7 Snapshots, for short
8 Cousin of an alpaca
9 Weather-affecting current
10 Place for a "Bridge Out" sign
11 Rock and Roll Hall of Fame architect
12 Like Fran Drescher's voice
13 Mournful peal
18 Have a hunch
22 Bit of equipment for a circus clown
23 Feudal drudges
24 Verboten
25 Burden of the conscience-stricken
26 Put on a pedestal
29 Attorney's org.
32 Event that may include blue films
34 Dirty campaign tactic
36 Bubbly drink
37 Protruding navel
38 Gaff, to a fisherman
40 Orator William Jennings ___
41 Rainbow shape
46 Dr. Phil's last name
48 Hip-shaking dance
50 Actor Leto of "American Psycho"
51 Chip away at
52 Choo-choo
53 Stacy who played Mike Hammer
55 Danger
57 Degs. for many profs
60 CAT scan alternative
61 A smoker might bum one
62 Trio after D
63 Kanga's baby

by Andrea Carla Michaels and Kent Clayton

ACROSS

1 Shade of green
5 Workplace watchdog, for short
9 "That ___ my question"
14 Each
15 Mrs. Frisby's charges in "The Secret of NIMH"
16 See 26-Across
17 Home of Eastern Michigan University
19 Rodeo rope
20 Harry Belafonte's specialty
22 "___ natural"
25 U.N. workers' grp.
26 One may be lit on a 16-Across
27 Veer off track
29 Pole, for one
31 It might precede a collection: Abbr.
32 Guns' partner
33 Rapper parodied by Weird Al Yankovic in "Amish Paradise"
35 1979 film with Capt. Willard and Col. Kurtz
40 Universally known
41 "Idylls of the King" lady
43 Motocross racer, for short
46 Skating maneuver
47 P.F.C.'s punishment
49 Some prayer clothing
51 My ___, Vietnam
52 ___-wolf
53 Undercover operatives . . . or what are hiding in 17-, 20-, 35- and 58-Across?
57 Onetime TWA competitor
58 Leaf-eating insect scourge

62 Hundredth: Prefix
63 Gray ___
64 Tot's injury
65 Couldn't stand
66 Garden divisions
67 Post-baby boomer group, for short

DOWN

1 Homer Simpson's middle name
2 iPad download, in brief
3 First of a pair of lists
4 Awesome
5 How some medications are taken
6 Big name in Japanese electronics
7 U.R.L. start
8 Sale condition
9 35-Across, for one
10 North Pacific islander
11 Immobility
12 Longtime local
13 Finder of missing persons
18 Cubs' place
21 Most toilet seats
22 Turkish title
23 Result of trauma, maybe
24 Pack (down)
28 Bark
29 Russian space program started in the 1960s
30 Takes the top (off)
33 Medical condition treated by thrombolysis
34 Lacking width and depth, for short
36 Screening aid

37 Something that can't be missed
38 Burden
39 ___ child (pregnant)
42 Hair salon stock
43 In and of itself
44 Title location in a Hemingway novel
45 Like rooms to rent
47 Where Manhattan is
48 Unfortunate circumstance
50 Correspond
51 Cartoon stinker
54 Food thickener
55 Greek deli specialty
56 Urban woe
59 Be short
60 Cookie holder
61 Do voodoo on

by Mike Nothnagel

ACROSS

1 Boeing 747s, e.g.
5 Out of bed for the day
10 Rand McNally product
13 Resting on
14 Part of the eye
15 In bed all day, maybe
16 Profits
18 Hornets' and Nuggets' org.
19 Industrial city of Germany
20 Winter precipitation
22 Gulf war missiles
25 Town dump, e.g.
28 Othello's supposed rival for Desdemona's affection
30 "Beep beep" maker
31 Commotion
32 Teacher, after exams
35 "Quickly!," on an order
39 The, grammatically
42 Musial of the Cardinals
43 Egyptian god of the underworld
44 Last in a sequence: Abbr.
45 ___ of Man
47 Actress Reynolds of "The Unsinkable Molly Brown"
49 Dodge City lawman
54 The "T" in TWA
55 German Hermann
56 Use the pink end of a pencil
58 Antlered animal
59 Emmy-winning nature series narrated by David Attenborough
65 Ginger ___

66 Grapefruit-like fruit
67 ___ as shootin'
68 Wrecker's job
69 Kick out of school
70 Shed thing hidden in 16-, 25-, 39-, 49- and 59-Across

DOWN

1 Feb. preceder
2 Summer in France
3 Tyke
4 Goes 80, say
5 Extend a subscription
6 Turner's 1986 rock autobiography
7 ___ City (Las Vegas)
8 London's locale: Abbr.
9 Former Egyptian leader with a lake named after him
10 Many a West Virginia worker
11 "The Zoo Story" playwright Edward
12 Oro y ___ (Montana's motto)
14 B&O and Short Line: Abbr.
17 Give, as homework
21 Island west of Maui
22 A lot
23 Citadel student
24 Stars and Stripes land, for short
26 Remove wool from
27 Hot
29 Baltimore baseballer
33 Bewildered
34 "Agnus ___"
36 Swim with the fishes, say
37 Bold poker bet
38 "For ___ sake!"

40 The J. and K. in J. K. Rowling: Abbr.
41 African fly pest
46 Vast treeless plain
48 Suckling site
49 Bread choice that's not white or rye
50 Mello ___ (soft drink)
51 Off-kilter
52 Actress Zellweger
53 Suave or VO5 competitor
57 From ___ Z
60 Bagel topper
61 What a guitar may be hooked up to
62 Regret
63 Gay singing syllable
64 Billy Joel's "Tell ___ About It"

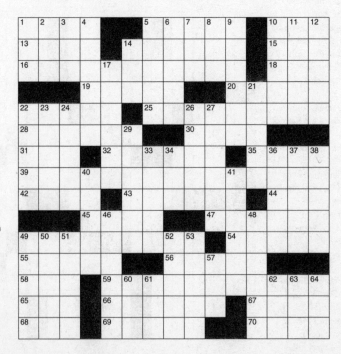

by Patrick Blindauer

ACROSS

1 End of a fable
6 Place to pray
9 Game with knights
14 Hitch on the run
15 "To a . . ." poem
16 8½"×14" paper size
17 Monica with two U.S. Open wins
18 Without reluctance
20 Make a legislative speech, e.g.
22 Ear doctor
23 Vote in favor
26 Go ballistic
30 Greedy person's cry before and after "all"
31 Get clean, as in rehab
32 No longer active: Abbr.
34 Catchall category
37 Popular cameras
39 Shade of green
40 Rapper's entourage
44 Choir voice
45 Be stir-crazy
49 "___ Ramsey" (1970s western)
50 "Pay to ___" (check words)
51 Where one might 20-, 26- and 45-Across?
57 Summer woe
60 ___ Jean (Marilyn, originally)
61 How the euphoric walk
62 They, in Tours
63 Bothered incessantly
64 Summer who sang "Love to Love You Baby"
65 Police dept. title
66 Performed superbly

DOWN

1 Go well together
2 Dairy case bar
3 See 11-Down
4 Mimicked
5 Anne Rice vampire
6 Propelled
7 Imposing building
8 Sturdily built
9 Advertising award
10 English king crowned in 1100
11 With 3-Down, Chinese restaurant offering
12 Mineo of film
13 On the ___ (furtively)
19 Hand moisturizer, e.g.
21 "Come again?"
24 Sign up
25 Ballplayers' representatives
26 Like state-of-the-art gadgetry
27 Get a lungful
28 Bit of gym attire
29 61, in old Rome
30 Swabbie's handful
33 General on Chinese menus
35 33⅓, for an LP
36 Tearful one
38 Penn of "Harold & Kumar" films
41 Olympian's no-no
42 Put in chains
43 Most weird
46 Strands during the winter, perhaps
47 Director Craven
48 Fight venues
52 More, in adspeak
53 "Letting Go" novelist Philip
54 Layered cookie
55 Neighbor of Yemen
56 9-Across ending
57 Cover with turf
58 Half of dos
59 A Bobbsey twin

by Mark Feldman

ACROSS

1 Friends and neighbors
5 Bend one's elbow, e.g.
9 Cornered
14 Start of an incantation
15 Wash up
16 "On the Beach" author
17 Hard-boiled crime genre
18 Aesir ruler
19 Perfect Sleeper maker
20 Athlete who has pigged out on snacks at a bar?
23 Interstate-championing prez
24 Strippers' tips, often
25 Explosive of old
28 Special treatment, for short
29 "___ geht's?" (German "How are you?")
30 ___ pro nobis
31 Chief heckler?
36 Skewer
37 Place for a Dumpster
38 Juan's "What"
39 Lavender, for one
40 Pesky arachnid
41 Skydiver's amended plans?
43 Troop-entertaining grp.
44 Cara ___ (Italian term of endearment)
45 Performer yukking it up
46 Friend from afar
48 Tickled
50 Indy letters
53 Insulation from jokes?
56 Rodeo ride
58 Astronomy's ___ cloud
59 Brand for woofers, but not tweeters?
60 Cultural prefix
61 Purple shade
62 Sound from a steeple
63 Core belief
64 Critic's unit
65 Primordial stuff

DOWN

1 Japanese writing system
2 Old Apple laptop
3 Brief moment
4 "Listen!," old-style
5 Walk with jerky motions
6 Chili server
7 Escapees from Pandora's box
8 Alien: Prefix
9 Take on
10 Angle symbol, in trigonometry
11 Explode like a puffball
12 "Boston Legal" fig.
13 Truly, in the Bible
21 Unwise undertaking
22 Brand once advertised with the jingle "We wear short shorts . . ."
26 Circular gasket
27 Barista's offering
28 Back into a corner
29 Boo-hoo
31 Copier malfunction
32 Beethoven dedicatee
33 "Rocket Man" rocker
34 Pastel hue
35 Scat syllable
36 Bernie Madoff's hedge fund, e.g.
39 Parasol's offering
41 Leave high and dry
42 Say "Hey, batter batter batter" and such
44 Mr. Met, for one
47 Tubular pasta
48 Mosaic artist's material
49 Spanish poet García ___
50 Fifth-century canonized pope
51 Birthstone for many Scorpios
52 Working stiff
54 The old man
55 Banjo accessory
56 Double or nothing, e.g.
57 Tpke., e.g.

by John Lampkin

ACROSS

1 Jump
5 1960s–'70s R&B singer Marilyn
10 Observe the Sabbath
14 Norway's capital
15 Thin as __
16 "Beetle Bailey" bulldog
17 Game played with strings looped over the fingers
19 Spicy Asian cuisine
20 Shaking a leg
21 Feather pen
22 Self-description of someone who's surprised
25 Farmer-turned-conman in a 1960s sitcom
28 Not much
29 Designer Geoffrey
30 Oklahoma city named for the daughter of its first 4-Down
31 Many miles off
35 Docs' org.
36 Long time
40 Hole in one
41 Song for one
43 Electrocute, in slang
44 Former name for Congo
46 Big hauler
48 Called balls and strikes
50 Taro
54 Bosc and Bartlett
55 Move to another job, say
59 Smarting
60 What a greedy person may grab
62 The "O" in CD-ROM
63 Disney mermaid
64 Prayer starter
65 Meal on a military base
66 Ashen, as a complexion
67 Blows away

DOWN

1 __ Ness monster
2 Biblical twin who sold his birthright
3 Cockpit readings: Abbr.
4 One who "always rings twice," in an old movie
5 Jarhead
6 Ill-tempered
7 Bum, as a cigarette
8 OPEC supply
9 Cheer for a toreador
10 Capitol feature
11 Body of values
12 Suddenly stop, as an engine
13 French fabric
18 Like Dolly the sheep
21 Sine __ non
23 When said three times, "and so on"
24 Fawn's father
25 Many corp. hirees
26 San __, Italian resort on the Mediterranean
27 "Physician, __ thyself"
30 Nile snake
32 Place to buy cotton candy
33 Farming unit
34 Wetlands plant
37 Princess in L. Frank Baum books
38 Loss's opposite
39 Modern toll-paying convenience
42 Fish-eating birds
45 Event for stunt pilots
47 Quizzical utterances
48 Early computer forum
49 Pathetically small
50 __ salts
51 Africa's Sierra __
52 Some English nobles
53 Un+deux
56 Othello's betrayer
57 "Oh, __ up!"
58 Nancy Drew's beau and others
60 Napkin's place
61 Savings for one's later years, for short

by Donna Hoke

ACROSS

1 Do a double-take, e.g.
6 Made a choice
11 Composition of Jack Haley's Oz character
14 God, to Muslims
15 Gaucho's plain
16 "Six Feet Under" network
17 F.A.A. supervisors?
19 Belief suffix
20 Start of a countdown
21 Jerome who composed "Ol' Man River"
22 Dolts
24 Object to online commentary?
27 Cosine's reciprocal
30 "Waiting for Lefty" playwright
31 It's walked on pirate ships
32 ". . . __ saw Elba"
34 Awaiting scheduling, initially
37 Holiday smokes?
41 Broadcast
42 Strong desires
43 Tickle
44 Want badly, with "for"
47 Least amiable
48 Cleaned up after a spill?
52 Tilter's weapon
53 __-Tass news agency
54 Martinique, par exemple
57 Heavenly body
58 Defamation in the Garden of Eden?
62 Fertility clinic cells
63 Potter's potions professor
64 Playing pieces in Rummikub
65 Nat Geo, for one
66 Snap course
67 Wield, as power

DOWN

1 Totally absorbed
2 Vogue competitor
3 Shepard in space
4 Pink-slip
5 "Lola" band
6 Start of grace, maybe
7 Fallback strategy
8 Subject of a cigarette rating
9 Shut down
10 Prescription measure
11 "You're right"
12 "The Wild Duck" playwright Henrik
13 Chinese restaurant request
18 Out of alignment
23 Bilko or Friday: Abbr.
24 Gershwin's "The __ Love"
25 Windblown soil
26 Keatsian or Pindaric
27 Pet advocacy org.
28 Grades K-12
29 Allotment of one, usually, for an airline passenger
32 Make improvements to
33 Turned chicken
35 One calling the shots
36 "I'd hate to break up __"
38 One of four on a Rolls
39 Cut jaggedly
40 Mideast potentate: Var.
45 Catchall abbr.
46 Free from anxiety
47 Font option: Abbr.
48 Burst into flower
49 Maggot or grub
50 Hardly macho
51 Totally lost
54 Pink-slip
55 Lecher's look
56 Once, old-style
59 Paternity suit evidence
60 Smallish batteries
61 Give a thumbs-down

by Alan Arbesfeld

ACROSS

1 *Cry at the start of a vote
6 Tree in California
10 Soulful Redding
14 Duane ___ (New York City pharmacy chain)
15 Land west of the Pacific
16 "This is terrible!"
17 Greased
18 "Believe" singer, 1999
19 Liberals, with "the"
20 *"Soon enough, my friend"
22 Big mess
24 "Bien ___!"
25 Former "S.N.L." comic Gasteyer
26 French theologian who wrote "Sic et Non"
28 Jean Sibelius, for one
29 Seat of Albany County, Wyo.
30 Biggie ___ (rapper a k a Notorious B.I.G.)
33 Bennett of "What's My Line?"
34 "Am ___ risk?"
35 Women's rights pioneer Elizabeth ___ Stanton
36 *As a package
37 Old man: Ger.
38 Here, in Juárez
39 Bomber type
41 More agile
43 Relinquish, as arms
45 Move from site to site?
46 Hall of TV fame
47 Oslo Accords party, for short
48 One way to sway
51 Many a Justin Bieber fan
52 *Completely imagined
54 Restaurateur Toots

55 Kirk's foe in a "Star Trek" sequel
57 Lofty dwelling
58 Unadulterated
59 Alveoli site
60 "I love you," in a telenovela
61 Sacred chests
62 Tense
63 Poker phrase . . . or what's needed to complete the answers to the six starred clues

DOWN

1 Aristophanes comedy, with "The"
2 Alphabetic pentad
3 Bravery
4 Took too much
5 Common North American hawk
6 Iconic chomper
7 New York stadium eponym
8 Taradiddle
9 Classic candy with nougat
10 "How lu-u-uxurious!"
11 *Top-rated TV series of 1971–76
12 Madden
13 Lush
21 Quaint lodgings
23 Brand of 45-Down balls
26 Direction at sea
27 Block
28 Pass muster
30 Where "Otello" premiered, with "La"
31 General played by Fonda (in 1976), Peck (1977) and Olivier (1982)
32 *To be expected
33 MSNBC competitor

36 Vintner's prefix
37 Terrier's sound
39 Exemplar of dryness
40 Glimmer
41 U.S.S. Enterprise helmsman
42 How some wages are calculated
44 Popular tractors
45 See 23-Down
48 Untamed
49 Sam who directed "Drag Me to Hell"
50 Classic theater
52 Masculine side
53 Cad
54 Where the robed are rubbed
56 Movie for which Patricia Neal won Best Actress

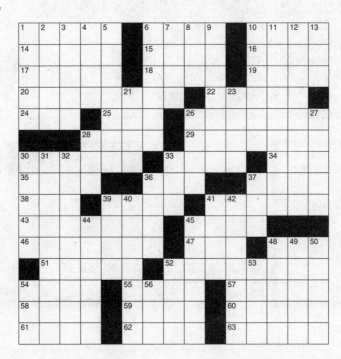

by Michael Sharp

The New York Times

SMART PUZZLES
PRESENTED WITH STYLE

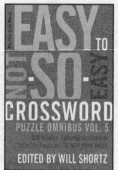

Available at your local bookstore or online at www.nytimes.com/nytstore

St. Martin's Griffin

1

```
N I N J A   A P L U S   T A B
A R I E S   B O O S T   E T A
G E T S O N E S W A Y   M D S
    U F O   S E T   C P A S
L E N S   T H E R O Y A L W E
E P A   N E O     D E C E N T
V I D E O   P O P A R T
I C A N T T E L L Y O U W H Y
    A I R S E A   U S A G E
S C A M P I     T N T   I T A
T A L E S O F W O E   A T V S
O V A L   X I I   H E R
L E S   P I T C H I N G W O O
I R K   E D U C E   D U B Y A
D N A   R E P A Y   S E A L S
```

2

```
A C D C   S P O C K   N D A K
T H O R   T I A R A   O I S E
T A M E   U N T I L   I S P Y
N I P S I N T H E B U D
    E S L   A S S   S E E R S
S H R I L L     L E A N I N
P A I D   I R O N E D   T A I
R I G A   R E I N A   K E L P
E R N   M A P L E S   E R T E
A D O R E S     E M P T O R
D O N E N   A C T   I T A
    J U G G L I N G P I N S
M A Z E   A R O M A   A N E W
A L E C   S E W E R   C E R A
P I N T   H E N R Y   E D D Y
```

3

```
A S H   V I S T A S   E L A N
C E O   A T T I L A   N A L A
C A A N   R E P E A L   T R A P
R I D D E R   A N A A L I C I A
A R O U S A L   I M E T
    S E T U P S   O L D I E
O B I T   I L A   S N E E Z Y
S A A B   D O U B L E A   S A A R
H E I D E N   L E G   P I K E
A D D E R   H O A R S E
    N E M O   N E O N A T E
A F R I K A A N S   G U N N E R
Q U I Z   L I A N A S   N A A N
U R G E   O N L A T E   I C I
A L A N   X G A M E S   E T E
```

4

```
M A R   S O B S   C O L T S
O B I   E R R O R   A C E I T
C I G A R C A S E   T H E T A
S T O V E   C A P E C O R A L
    L E N A   D O R A   S N L
C U E C A R D     I L K
H S T   C O A T C L O S E T
I S T O   U M A   S P C A
C R O P C I R C L E   A R F
    T A D   C R E W C U T
S H O   R O D S   A L I E
C A M E C L E A N   E N S U E
O S A K A   C L A Y C O U R T
O T H E R   K A P U T   I G O
T E A S E   D A M S   T E N
```

5

```
L A P T O P   N E W S   R I M
O B E Y E R   A C H Y   A L E
L O C K D E V I C E S   B I N
L U K E   F E V E R   M B A S
    S P A R E   E R O I C A
A V A   R B S   T I L T
C I R C U S A C R O B A T S
T E C H S   C O E   C R E P E
  W H I S K E Y G L A S S E S
    I L I E   A I G   T D S
O U T L A Y   U L C E R
P R E Y   C U R I E   A L A S
T I C   J A C K A N D J I L L
E A T   I S L E   S C A M P I
D H S   M E A L   E C H O E D
```

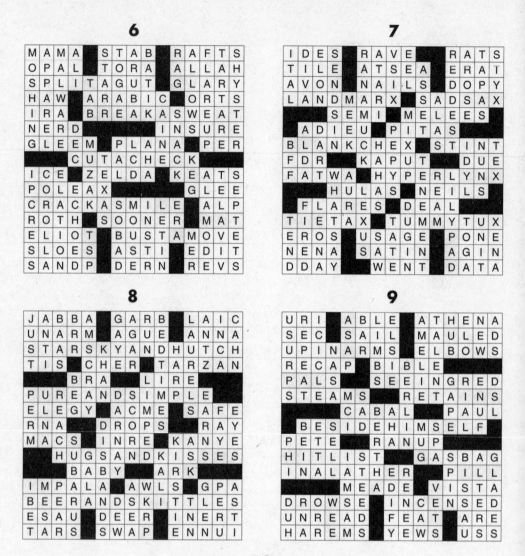

6

```
MAMA  STAB  RAFTS
OPAL  TORA  ALLAH
SPLITAGUT  GLARY
HAW ARABIC  ORTS
IRA BREAKASWEAT
NERD     INSURE
GLEEM PLANA  PER
    CUTACHECK
ICE ZELDA  KEATS
POLEAX     GLEE
CRACKASMILE ALP
ROTH SOONER  MAT
ELIOT BUSTAMOVE
SLOES ASTI  EDIT
SANDP DERN  REVS
```

7

```
IDES  RAVE  RATS
TILE  ATSEA ERAT
AVON  NAILS DOPY
LANDMARX  SADSAX
  SEMI  MELEES
  ADIEU  PITAS
BLANKCHEX  STINT
FDR  KAPUT  DUE
FATWA  HYPERLYNX
  HULAS  NEILS
  FLARES  DEAL
TIETAX  TUMMYTUX
EROS  USAGE  PONE
NENA  SATIN  AGIN
DDAY  WENT  DATA
```

8

```
JABBA  GARB  LAIC
UNARM  AGUE  ANNA
STARSKYANDHUTCH
TIS CHER  TARZAN
  BRA  LIRE
PUREANDSIMPLE
ELEGY ACME  SAFE
RNA DROPS  RAY
MACS INRE  KANYE
  HUGSANDKISSES
  BABY  ARK
IMPALA AWLS  GPA
BEERANDSKITTLES
ESAU DEER  INERT
TARS SWAP  ENNUI
```

9

```
URI ABLE  ATHENA
SEC SAIL  MAULED
UPINARMS  ELBOWS
RECAP  BIBLE
PALS  SEEINGRED
STEAMS  RETAINS
  CABAL  PAUL
  BESIDEHIMSELF
PETE  RANUP
HITLIST  GASBAG
INALATHER  PILL
  MEADE  VISTA
DROWSE  INCENSED
UNREAD FEAT  ARE
HAREMS YEWS  USS
```

10

```
ISLE  BALMY  TBSP
DIET  ILIAD  RATA
INTHEDUMPS  IRAS
 TIER  MOO  DARNS
PATROL  UTILIZE
AXL DOWNTHEROAD
PEI EPEE  EDU
ASEA  BIT  NYPD
  IAN  GRAB  OLE
OVERTHEHILL  GEL
TEABALL  FACIAL
OCTAD  OHS  NABS
OTIS UPTHECREEK
LONE  METOO  LADY
ERGS  ASPEN  AROD
```

11

S	I	P	S		H	U	S	H		I	N	F	E	R
C	O	A	L		O	H	I	O		N	E	I	G	H
A	N	N	A		N	O	L	O		F	A	R	G	O
M	I	D	N	I	G	H	T	H	O	U	R			
S	C	A	T	S			A	T	T		S	H	A	
		M	A	T	T	H	O	U	S	T	O	N		
M	A	M	A		R	O	O		R	O	A	S	T	
A	P	A	R	T	M	E	N	T	H	O	U	S	E	S
M	I	N	C	E		T	A	E		S	H	A	Y	
B	A	S	S	E	T	H	O	U	N	D				
O	N	E		S	H	E		O	U	T	D	O		
		W	H	E	R	E	A	R	T	T	H	O	U	
C	A	P	R	I		B	L	U	E		U	R	N	S
S	W	E	A	R		A	S	K	S		R	O	U	T
I	N	A	P	T		L	E	S	T		N	E	T	S

12

A	G	A	P	E		A	D	Z	E		A	G	A	S
S	O	L	O	S		D	R	E	S	S	R	A	C	K
S	T	O	P	P	E	D	O	N	A	P	E	N	N	Y
O	T	O			X	I	S			A	W	G	E	E
C	A	P	T	A	I	N	S	D	I	M	E	S		
		A	F	T			A	M	S		I	C	I	
H	O	O	H	A		V	E	R	A		E	G	A	D
I	N	C	O	R	R	E	C	T	C	H	A	N	G	E
L	U	C	E		E	R	O	S		A	T	S	E	A
L	S	U		O	A	S			S	H	E			
		P	U	M	P	E	R	Q	U	A	R	T	E	R
A	M	A	N	A		O	A	F			I	L	E	
P	I	N	C	H	I	N	G	N	I	C	K	E	L	S
A	C	C	L	A	I	M	E	D		E	E	R	I	E
R	A	Y	E		N	I	T	A		O	N	S	E	T

13

S	P	A	T		I	T	C	H		S	L	A	S	H
H	E	S	S		N	E	H	I		C	O	P	T	O
A	R	I	A		H	A	I	L		O	A	S	I	S
Q	U	A	R	T	E	R	P	O	U	N	D	E	R	S
			H	R	S			S	E	E				
A	D	M	I	R	E		F	L	U		D	A	T	E
B	U	E	N	O		B	O	A	R		D	U	A	L
H	A	L	F	B	L	O	O	D	P	R	I	N	C	E
O	N	E	I		O	R	L	Y		A	C	T	I	N
R	E	E	D		R	E	S		F	I	E	S	T	A
			E	O	N			P	A	S				
F	U	L	L	M	E	T	A	L	J	A	C	K	E	T
U	S	A	I	N		E	S	A	I		R	A	R	A
D	E	N	T	I		L	E	S	T		A	M	I	S
D	R	A	Y	S		L	A	M	A		B	A	C	K

14

V	I	A	L		T	O	D	D	L	E		M	A	R
A	C	L	U		H	E	R	E	O	N		A	M	I
C	H	I	C	K	E	N	Y	A	R	D		R	I	M
				C	A	W		E	R	N		I	O	N	S
D	I	G	I	T	A	L	Y	E	A	R	B	O	O	K
O	N	O		S	L	I	E	R		E	E	N	S	Y
O	D	O	M		R	N	S		C	P	A			
R	O	P	E	R	U	G		T	O	O	M	A	N	Y
			T	I	S		T	R	U		S	L	A	V
P	I	P	I	T		H	E	I	N	Z		E	S	E
A	N	I	M	A	L	I	N	S	T	I	N	C	T	S
L	U	X	E		E	T	A		R	O	E			
A	R	I		C	A	T	C	H	I	N	A	L	I	E
C	E	E		A	V	E	R	S	E		L	A	M	E
E	D	S		B	E	R	E	T	S		E	X	P	O

15

P	E	A	C	E		B	O	I	S		E	B	A	Y
A	T	L	A	S		O	N	C	E		M	I	N	E
T	H	E	T	A		S	T	E	T		A	C	O	W
E	A	R	C	U	T	S	O	L	U	T	I	O	N	
	N	T	H		D	E	P		P	O	L	A		
		A	S	S	D	I	S	M	I	S	S	E	D	
A	M	O	L	E		C	P	A		T	Z	E		
D	U	L	L	A	R	D		A	N	T	F	A	R	M
I	N	D		E	R	R		K	O	L	A	S		
A	I	M	S	A	D	J	U	S	T	O	R			
	A	A	N	D		S	E	N		E	D	O		
	A	S	H	O	F	T	H	E	T	I	T	A	N	S
A	C	T	A		O	R	D	S		N	O	F	E	E
B	R	E	R		X	I	I	I		C	L	O	U	T
S	E	R	A		X	M	E	N		A	D	E	P	T

16

```
A R R R   C R O P     A P P S
N O A H   L O V E S   R O O T
D A V Y J O N E S L O C K E R
I R I S E S   R E A M   E M U
      L E A S T   A V A S T
T A L K L I K E A   H E R
A T O I   N I E   M A G O G
B A S S O O N   P E N G U I N
  D E M O N   P A D   I N G A
  N E C   P I R A T E D A Y
B O O T Y   A N K L E
A C T   T I C K   L A A L A A
S H I V E R M E T I M B E R S
I R M A   S A Y S O   B A C H
N E E T   N E O N   A H O Y
```

17

```
C P U S   A P I A   L U C A S
A L P E   N A C L   E R O D E
B U D G E T C U T   A I R E R
A R A   C O M   I N A N
N A T I O N A L A N T H E M S
A L E C   N O A H   S L A W
  E G G   U R A L   I R A
D O L L A R D I P L O M A C Y
A V E   D U E S   F L O
D E F T   M A X I   J E N A
E N T E R P R I S E Z O N E S
  W H E Y   O X O   L A K
A K I R A   R E N T A C A R S
S O N A R   A L T O   A C T I
S I G N S   F O O L   P E O N
```

18

```
Z E B U   A R Y A N S   M C A
I R A N   R E E D I T   I A N
G A R D E N G R O V E   D V D
    E L O I   E R A S E R
P U R R S   O C E A N S I D E
E M U S   I N O N   U Z I S
U P B E A T   R U M P   E N S
  B A K E R S F I E L D
O P E   A M I E   S A U C E S
F I R S   C T R S   N A S H
S A N T A R O S A   T E R S E
O N E D G E   M A R T
R I C   I N N E R C I T I E S
T S K   L I E S O N   E T T A
S T S   E N C O D E   S T A X
```

19

```
P A W   F L O O D   I G I V E
A H A   L A T T E   A L O E S
R O L L O V E R M I N U T E S
T Y K E   L O O P   T A S E
    G A O L   R O V E
    S I T D O W N D I N N E R
E N C O R E   O A S T   O V A
P O R N O   D R Y   I D T A G
I N A   P S I S   A A R O N S
C O M E H E R E O F T E N
    L Y R E   B R E A
P U M A   I N E S   M A G I
S T A Y O F E X E C U T I O N
S A U N A   E P S O N   D O G
T H I E F   D O S E S   A D E
```

20

```
I B I S   C L U E   E P S O M
S A M M Y C A H N   T R A C E
A D M I S S I O N   H O S T A
S M E L L   C H A K A K H A N
  I D E     O N E A L S
A N I S E   M A S K E D
U T A   S H I N T O   S M E W
T O T   C O N G A M E   O X O
O N E G   M I L T O N   N I K
    R E E S E S   A S S T S
E S S E N E     O I S
J A M E S C A A N   A L G I D
E R I T U   F R E E R A N G E
C A T E R   B I L L Y C O N N
T H E R E   S A L K   E R S T
```

21

```
SPY    DAUBS   PEWS
ALES   ITSOK   IHOP
NATUREVSNURTURE
KNIVES   RELOADED
    SUDS    SKY
SHE  POLE   SAVAGE
MANVSWILD   LARAS
ASTI   NEVIS   TAMP
STEVE   RENTVSBUY
HERALD   RARA   STS
    FRY   HAND
WOOKIEES   TERESA
ALIENVSPREDATOR
VENN   INCOG   BAUM
YOKO   LOAMY   SPY
```

22

```
CLASPS   HBO   YODA
HACKIT   ARP   ALIT
ESTATE   NAE   MERV
WESTVIRGINIA
SRO   INRUN   RHEIN
   SNAP   SPITVALVE
      HEM   SAO   LAW
DISHRAG   CLEMENS
ASA   ROS   DXI
SPLITVOTE   IGOR
HYENA   DIDST   LAY
   ABSOLUTVODKA
THAW   AMT   RIPPER
VIVA   FEE   USERID
SPAY   END   TALONS
```

23

```
TALC   MESA   ATTA
AREA   EAGER   IRAS
TRAVELCARD   RIMS
   ING   DIE   FAIT
JESTERS   ONCALL
ALLY   ETC   TARP
BIO   SCARF   REEKS
OTT   ZONEOUT   RAW
TEMPE   STOKE   INE
   ALLS   EDU   SOYA
SCALED   SLANDER
DAHS   LOP   ETA
EXIT   DOUBLETIME
CONE   OZZIE   COAX
ONER   MYOB   HUGO
```

24

```
MESS   STAPLE   CPU
EXPO   TERROR   HAG
THEBOUNCINGBALL
ROE   ANTON   ARMY
ORDERS   CAPRA
STYX   THELEADER
   OSSIA   TAKETO
OVA   THATCAR   SEZ
JAGUAR   EARLY
ONESHEART   SORT
   GELDS   FOLLOW
ZERO   KARAT   DEI
INONESFOOTSTEPS
NYU   ROOKIE   ASET
GAP   APRILS   ITRY
```

25

```
QTIPS   APES   GLOB
TOTAL   JUMP   ROTE
SUCRE   AMIR   ANTE
 THEPURPLEONION
   NTH   END
SPAT   OPENSESAME
HIS   SHARI   ROLEX
EXTRA   PIT   UNITE
LEROI   ACTIN   BAR
FLOODPLAIN   SILT
   TAR   CEL
THEWHOLESHMEAR
AUTO   BEVY   BAGEL
KERR   EVEN   EZINE
EYED   DISC   DENTS
```

26

M	A	W		L	E	C	T	O	R		C	R	O	P
A	B	E		A	L	C	O	V	E		A	U	D	I
S	R	I		C	L	I	V	E	B	A	R	N	E	S
S	I	R	R	E	E			R	A	N	D	D		
E	D	D	B	Y	R	N	E	S		N	O	O	N	E
U	G	L	I			O	L	E	O		O	W	E	N
R	E	Y		M	I	L	L	E	B	O	R	N	E	S
			D	O	T				I	R	S			
D	A	V	I	D	B	I	R	N	E	Y		R	A	T
I	K	E	A		E	A	S	E		C	O	C	O	
P	A	R	M	A		S	T	B	E	R	N	A	R	D
	M	A	R	I	S			L	A	N	D	E	D	
F	R	O	N	T	B	U	R	N	E	R		M	A	L
A	I	N	T		I	M	D	O	N	E		A	G	E
N	O	T	E		S	E	A	W	A	R		P	E	R

27

L	A	P	P		S	O	D	A	S			I	N	M	Y
O	D	O	R		T	R	O	L	L			C	O	D	E
C	A	L	I	F	O	R	N	I	A	G	I	R	L	S	
I	M	O	V	E	R	I	T		T	E	C				
			A	D	E	N			H	E	L	P	M	E	
P	L	A	T	O	S		W	O	E		E	L	A	L	
R	A	K	E	R		B	O	H	R			D	A	R	T
O	V	I		A	M	O	R	I	S	T		T	K	O	
P	I	N	S		A	C	R	O		W	A	T	E	R	
E	S	T	A		N	A	Y		B	O	L	E	R	O	
R	H	O	N	D	A			A	R	A	B				
			C	O	G		B	R	O	C	A	D	E	S	
L	I	T	T	L	E	S	A	I	N	T	N	I	C	K	
A	B	O	U		R	A	B	A	T		I	A	T	E	
R	O	O	M		S	T	Y	N	E		A	L	O	E	

28

G	A	G		F	E	E	L	I	N		S	E	E	D
R	T	E		U	P	D	A	T	E		A	L	L	Y
O	T	T		R	I	G	H	T	T	O	L	I	F	E
W	H	O	A		L	E	T		S	P	A			
L	E	F	T	T	O	D	I	E		E	M	B	E	D
		F	R	O	G		V	A	N	I	L	L	A	
A	S	T	I	R		S	A	I	D			A	L	F
S	T	R	A	I	G	H	T	T	O	V	I	D	E	O
O	L	A		T	A	M	E		I	R	E	N	E	
R	E	C	R	O	O	M		B	E	A	R			
T	O	K	E	N		U	P	T	O	S	N	U	F	F
		K	I	D		L	E	A		I	N	R	E	
D	O	W	N	T	O	E	A	R	T	H		N	A	T
O	L	I	O		D	E	C	R	E	E		E	M	U
E	D	I	T		O	L	E	A	R	Y		R	E	S

29

S	A	W	T	O		C	A	M	P		L	A	T	H
I	M	E	A	N		O	B	O	E		E	U	R	O
C	O	B	R	A		R	I	D	E		S	P	A	R
		S	P	R	I	N	T	E	R	U	S	A	I	N
A	L	I		O	N	E			S	E	I	N	E	
M	E	T	A	L	F	A	S	T	E	N	E	R		
O	N	E	A	L			L	O	L	A				
S	A	S	H		A	L	O	O	F		T	C	B	Y
			A	S	I	A			E	R	A	S	E	
	L	I	G	H	T	N	I	N	G	U	N	I	T	
S	T	O	N	E			N	E	G		D	X	I	
L	E	A	V	E	S	U	D	D	E	N	L	Y		
U	L	N	A		T	R	E	E		O	O	M	P	H
S	L	E	D		O	G	L	E		G	R	A	C	E
H	Y	D	E		W	E	L	D		S	E	N	S	E

30

X	M	A	S		R	A	D	A	R	S		P	A	T
R	A	I	L		U	N	C	L	E	S		O	R	E
A	T	R	O	P	H	Y	C	A	S	E		R	T	E
Y	A	B	B	E	R		A	M	I		A	T	I	T
L	H	A	S	A		E	B	O	N	Y	F	I	S	H
A	A	S		L	A	V			E	L	A	T	E	
B	R	E	A		C	A	R	D	I	A	C			
	I	S	L	A	N	D	E	R	T	R	I	A	L	
		C	R	E	E	P	I	N		O	L	E	O	
A	L	L	O	T			F	O	G		E	A	R	
O	L	I	V	E	B	A	I	T		M	A	U	N	A
L	A	T	E		A	N	D		W	A	N	T	O	N
E	M	T		U	N	I	T	P	I	C	K	I	N	G
R	A	E		R	E	M	A	I	N		L	A	M	E
S	S	R		U	S	A	G	E	S		E	N	E	S

31

```
S C O O P | C R A B | A L S O
C O N G A | R O P E | C I A O
R O A R S | A L E C | A M M O
A P P E T I Z E R O R D E R |
P E A | O N E | T O O | R A P
E R R O R S | B U L B | I I I
| S A U C E R | A C M E
| B I L L M A Z E R O S K I
C O M O | L O S E R S
S T P | A W L S | F A N N E D
I S O | O A S | L E T | A L I
| W U R L I T Z E R O R G A N
Z A N E | T I E D | R E S I N
I N D O | O M N I | I N A N E
P A S S | N E O N | O T T E R
```

32

```
C R O P | I M A C | T I L E D
L E C H | N A I L | E R A S E
I D E A | G O T O H E A V E N
C H A S M | C R A T E |
H O N E Y I M H O M E | I F S
E T S | E G O | X M R A D I O
| K Y O T O | D I N O
| T O W E R O F L O N D O N |
M A M A | T A P A S
I P A N E M A | D A D | F D A
T E N | K I T T Y L I T T E R
| O B E S E | R E R A N
H I D D E N T E X T | N O N E
A D E E R | U N I S | D O N S
N O M S G | D Y N E | S P A S
```

33

```
C H E N | M A R S | P S H A W
R O T A | A T O P | I P A N A
I W A S | N C A A | X A N A X
M A L L E T O R C L A W |
E R I | Q A S | E A R N I N G
A D I E U | T A M I | N O M
| R A J | P E R I O D I C
W R I G L E Y A N D C O O R S
A E R O S T A R | S I N |
I N A | S R T A | C A B I N
F E E L B A D | R E L | A N Y
| L I M A O R L E N T I L
M Y B A D | R B I S | O H T O
B E A M E | M O V E | R E I N
A W M A N | S E E S | A D O S
```

34

```
H I G H | M E N S A | F I L L
O N E A | A S S A M | I D L E
C O T T O N S W A B | S T A N
K I T | T E A | B I G H A N D
| L O V E D I T | L E G O S
| K E R | I D E E S |
R U N N I N G M A T E | P S I
A V O N | I N E R T | A L A N
J A W | C R A C K E R J A C K
| P H O T O | I A N |
S P O R E | P I T C R E W
P I N E T A R | C E E | F I G
A X I S | K O S H E R S A L T
R I O T | I B E A M | A R L O
K E N O | N E W T S | S E A S
```

35

```
M A I A | A J A R | T H I E F
I S B N | C O N E | C Y C L O
T H E G R E A T P U M P K I N
T O L E T | D E A N | N Y E T
S T I L E S | Y U G O
| E A S T L A | M O T T O S
A T V | A A B A | B I A L Y
T H E F U N K Y C H I C K E N
M A S A I | E S C E | E S C
S T O L E N | S T E F F I
| L S A T | L I O T T A
I S P S | V A S E | D R E A R
T H E F L Y I N G T O M A T O
C A N O E | N O G O | A S A S
H Y D R A | T W O D | L Y R E
```

36

W	E	E	B			T	B	A	R			E	P	S	O	M
U	C	L	A			H	O	R	A			M	I	N	G	O
S	T	E	A	M	R	O	O	M			I	G	O	R	S	
S	O	M	B	R	E	R	O			A	L	L	W	E	T	
				A	S	E				B	R	E	A			
S	C	R	A	P	P	A	P	E	R			T	V	A	D	
T	R	E			E	M	I	R	S			L	I	E	T	O
R	O	L	F	E			R	O	T			O	N	R	E	D
I	W	I	L	L			W	O	O	E	R			S	I	G
P	E	T	A			W	A	F	F	L	E	C	O	N	E	
			T	H	E	Y				E	L	O				
A	B	A	S	E	D			L	O	V	E	R	B	O	Y	
B	U	X	O	M			F	I	V	E	I	R	O	N	S	
B	R	E	D	A			A	M	I	N			A	D	E	E
A	L	L	A	N			D	A	D	S			L	E	A	R

37

E	T	A	I	L			T	E	S	H			N	A	T	O
A	E	T	N	A			A	N	T	E			A	L	I	T
S	L	E	E	T			P	T	A	S			F	O	N	T
T	E	M	P	O	R	A	R	Y	T	A	T	T	O	O		
			T	Y	E					I	O	T	A			
A	L	T			A	N	T	E	N	N	A			S	T	A
R	I	O	T			T	O	V				R	I	T	A	S
T	E	N	N	E	S	S	E	E	T	I	T	A	N	S		
S	U	E	T	S				N	T	H			S	T	Y	E
Y	T	D			T	E	E	T	H	E	S			S	A	T
			S	E	T	A				F	T	D				
T	E	E	T	E	R	T	O	T	T	E	R	I	N	G		
H	T	T	P			A	S	T	O			P	O	S	I	T
A	T	T	A			D	A	R	T			P	I	N	T	O
T	A	U	T			E	T	A	S			E	T	T	E	S

38

B	I	N	S			A	V	O	N			U	M	B	E	R
I	S	E	E			R	A	G	U			S	T	I	L	E
B	A	R	N	A	C	L	E	C	H	E	S	T	E	D		
S	O	F	T	C			E	L	O			I	S	M	S	
			C	H	O	C			E	R	I	N				
	S	C	O	T	C	H	P	I	N	N	A	C	L	E		
W	A	R	D			T	E	A				T	I	L	E	D
O	S	O			T	O	R	N	A	D	O			A	G	A
O	H	W	O	W			D	O	E			F	R	O	M	
F	A	N	N	I	E	M	A	N	A	C	L	E	S			
			E	T	T	A			E	L	H	I				
M	O	A	N			U	R	N				E	E	R	I	E
A	D	D	A	P	I	N	C	H	O	F	S	A	L	T		
G	I	Z	M	O			E	A	S	T			B	R	I	C
S	N	E	E	R			R	A	T	S			Y	E	A	H

39

P	O	E	M			H	U	S	H			S	P	I	E	L
A	L	A	I			A	R	I	A			P	I	N	K	O
P	E	R	K			M	I	L	L			A	N	G	E	L
	S	P	E	C	I	A	L	F	O	R	C	E	S			
			M	O	T	H			A	S	H					
A	R	E	Y	O	U			S	A	T	E			N	B	C
F	E	V	E	R	P	I	T	C	H			C	O	R	A	
R	E	A	R	S			R	E	M			J	O	N	E	S
O	D	D	S			L	I	V	E	R	E	M	O	T	E	
S	S	E			B	A	S	E			A	T	E	S	T	S
			S	R	I				G	I	L	A				
	S	A	T	U	R	D	A	Y	N	I	G	H	T			
H	U	N	A	N			E	B	R	O			A	I	R	S
A	R	T	I	E			A	L	O	U			I	D	E	A
H	E	I	D	I			R	E	S	T			N	E	E	D

40

P	O	N	D	E	R			D	A	N			G	E	N	S
P	R	I	O	R	I			A	L	E			A	B	E	T
P	U	P	P	E	T	S	H	O	W			M	O	R	E	
			A	C	U	T	L	E	T	A	B	O	V	E		
A	R	T			T	A	Y				H	I	K	E	R	
L	O	O	S	E	L	E	A	F	L	E	T					
I	N	K	E	D				P	O	E	M			S	A	G
E	D	E	N			P	A	R	E	D			W	A	G	E
N	O	N			M	I	N	I				S	H	I	R	E
			R	I	N	G	L	E	T	T	O	N	E	S		
T	R	E	E	S				S	U	R			T	E	E	
E	A	V	E	S	D	R	O	P	L	E	T					
E	T	A	L			R	A	I	N	S	T	O	R	M	S
T	I	D	E			A	I	L			A	T	O	N	A	L
H	O	E	D			Y	D	S			N	O	T	A	R	Y

41

```
M E G A ■ A P P ■ A D L I B S
A L I T ■ F E U ■ D E T O U R
R A zz M A T A zz ■ J A C U zz I
C I A ■ M A R L B O R O ■ ■
O N R Y E ■ S E R I ■ L O F T
S E D E R S ■ ■ I N G ■ G R E
■ ■ N I C K E D ■ E E R I E
■ C A T C H I N G S O M E zz
J O L L A ■ S T E L M O ■ ■
A S P ■ N I M ■ R E T A G S
zz T O P ■ N E W S ■ T E R R A
■ ■ I M I T A T O R ■ T I N
Q U I zz E D ■ F U zz Y W U zz Y
B A C A L L ■ E P I ■ A R L O
S W I zz L E ■ R E E ■ R O Y S
```

42

```
C O O P S ■ E K E S ■ I B E T
A C H O O ■ T A L K ■ N E M O
B E A R W I T H M E ■ S T I R
L A R K ■ P A N E L ■ E T T E
E N A C T S ■ ■ R E P A Y ■
■ ■ H O O T S ■ T O M B O Y
A M N O T ■ E P S O M ■ O N A
L O O P ■ B R O W N ■ D O C K
E T S ■ C L A R A ■ W I P E S
S H E R P A ■ E P S O N ■ ■
■ ■ D A R C Y ■ T O O H O T
F A I R ■ K O A L A ■ S O L O
L I V E ■ S U G A R D A D D Y
I D E S ■ O R E O ■ A U G I E
P A S T ■ X E R S ■ B R E E D
```

43

```
E R E C T ■ O D E S ■ T I C K
S U S H I ■ U R S A ■ W I R E
S E Q U E N T I A L ■ I N O N
■ T R A D E ■ O R S O N
R I T Z ■ B O R D E R L I N E
A D A P T S ■ E T D ■ S E D
T O R A H ■ I N A N E ■ T R Y
■ H E A D S T A R T ■
Z I P ■ A L L A H ■ E A T U P
A D E ■ T O E ■ E D M O N D
M I N O R E R R O R ■ P O O F
B A D G E ■ E V I T A ■
O M A R ■ B R E A K A B L E S
N I N E ■ L A S T ■ C A I R O
I N T S ■ T H E E ■ T Y P E D
```

44

```
R O T C ■ K N O T ■ S A G A S
A S E A ■ A C N E ■ P L A T E
P L U M B T R E E ■ A L G E R
T O T E R M ■ S A M I A M B
■ L O A F S ■ S S N ■
L L D ■ C N O T E S ■ A B B A
A A A ■ A D R A W ■ P L E A S
D U M B D U M B B U L L E T S
E R N I E ■ A L A N A ■ P I A
S A S S ■ S T E N T S ■ S K Y
■ C L U ■ S K I T S ■
B E Q U I E T ■ M E A N I E
L I E I N ■ P A P E R J A M B
E R I T U ■ K I E L ■ A S I A
W E I S S ■ E D G Y ■ K A T Y
```

45

```
D R O P ■ B A S E R ■ A G A S
R A V E ■ A C C R A ■ E L L A
J E A N S S M A R T ■ R E I N
■ A H E M ■ F I A N C E
D O G G I E S ■ V I N T N E R
E R R A N D ■ M I N C E S ■
L E A P T ■ W O N K A ■ C H I
V O C E ■ D A R N S ■ G L A D
E S E ■ G U T S Y ■ M O O R E
■ S T A N C E ■ S I E S T A
I P S W I C H ■ P O S S E S S
P O L I T E ■ T A U T ■
O D I N ■ C H I C S Y O U N G
D I C E ■ A I M E E ■ A S I A
S A K S ■ P E E R S ■ K E P T
```

46

B	I	L	B	O		B	M	O	C	S		A	M	A
A	S	I	A	N		E	A	R	T	H		N	I	P
B	U	T	T	E	R	F	L	Y	S	H	R	I	M	P
A	Z	T		S	O	O	T			E	M	I	L	
R	U	L	E		C	R	A	W	L	S	P	A	C	E
	E	R	A	S	E		E	A	T	A				
O	M	E	N	S			D	E	C	A	Y	I	N	G
R	E	V		S	T	R	O	K	E	S		D	I	E
I	R	A	N	I	A	N	S		I	R	E	N	E	
	O	S	S	A		R	E	S	I	N				
B	A	C	K	I	S	S	U	E	S		A	T	O	N
A	G	R	I		N	A	T	O		I	P	O		
B	R	E	A	S	T	O	F	C	H	I	C	K	E	N
Y	E	T		A	W	A	I	T		L	O	I	R	E
S	E	E		P	A	R	T	S		S	E	T	A	T

47

M	A	L	A	Y		D	E	B		I	R	A	T	E
A	M	O	L	E		E	P	A		N	E	X	U	S
R	O	S	E	S		R	I	A		D	I	E	T	S
L	E	I	F	E	R	I	C	S	S	O	N			
I	B	N		S	I	D			I	N	E	R	T	
N	A	G	S		C	E	L	I	N	E	D	I	O	N
	H	A	H			O	N	E	S			B	T	U
P	R	E	S	I	D	E	N	T	W	I	L	S	O	N
I	T	A		G	R	E	G			A	S	P		
P	E	R	I	H	E	L	I	O	N		D	R	A	W
	S	T	R	A	D			S	O	S		E	R	E
		O	L	D	M	A	C	D	O	N	A	L	D	
G	A	U	N	T		O	V	A		L	A	D	E	D
A	P	N	E	A		O	E	R		I	L	E	N	E
S	T	A	R	R		S	R	S		D	A	R	E	D

48

L	O	L	A		S	E	E	S	A	W		D	E	S
I	M	A	C		S	T	R	O	K	E		A	L	L
P	I	T	C	H	E	S	A	F	I	T		F	I	E
O	T	E	R	I		S	A	T		O	O	Z	E	
	C	A	T	C	H	E	S	A	B	R	E	A	K	
G	O	O		S	H	E			S	O	N			
A	L	M	A		A	M	I	S		P	A	B	L	O
F	I	E	L	D	S	A	Q	U	E	S	T	I	O	N
F	O	R	M	A		N	S	E	C		E	G	G	Y
	O	N	T		D	O	M		T	E	X			
B	A	T	S	A	N	E	Y	E	L	A	S	H		
R	I	O	T		O	L	E		M	A	R	I	A	
U	S	A		S	T	E	A	L	S	A	K	I	S	S
I	L	S		H	E	N	R	Y	S		E	L	L	A
N	E	T		A	S	A	S	E	T		S	L	A	P

49

C	A	W	S		W	O	O	L		B	I	P	E	D
A	S	I	T		I	N	K	Y		U	T	E	R	O
R	I	F	E		N	O	R	M		S	E	A	R	S
P	A	I	R	A	G	R	A	P	H	S		R	O	E
			E	N	S			H	I	T	H	A	R	D
H	O	P	O	N	P	O	P		D	O	O	M		
O	R	E		S	A	T	I	N		P	L	O	W	S
C	A	R	B		N	O	P	A	R		D	U	A	L
K	N	E	A	D		S	E	P	I	A		N	N	E
	A	R	R	S		D	E	P	L	E	T	E	D	
S	A	M	B	A	E	D			A	P	U			
P	L	O		P	A	R	E	A	P	H	R	A	S	E
A	C	U	T	E		A	D	D	A		O	K	A	Y
C	O	R	E	R		M	E	I	R		P	I	N	E
E	A	S	E	S		A	N	A	T		E	N	D	S

50

R	E	A	R	M		B	A	B	E		I	L	E	S
A	N	G	E	R	M	A	N	A	G	E	M	E	N	T
R	O	A	D	T	O	S	I	N	G	A	P	O	R	E
E	L	I	S		O	R	G		S	T	E	N	O	S
R	A	N		L	A	H	R			L	E	N		
		B	A	A		T	O	P	P	S				
A	T	E	A	M		A	G	A	R		T	I	C	
L	A	S	T	P	I	C	T	U	R	E	S	H	O	W
O	N	T	H	E	W	A	T	E	R	F	R	O	N	T
T	K	O		R	O	T	H			A	T	R	A	S
	H	E	N	C	E		W	B	A					
	A	B	O		H	O	C	H		T	O	A		
O	L	E	O	L	E		P	I	A		L	O	C	H
H	O	R	T	O	N	H	E	A	R	S	A	W	H	O
T	H	E	C	O	L	O	R	O	F	M	O	N	E	Y
O	A	T	H		S	E	A	S		U	S	E	R	S

51

SETUP SAPOR ETE
ADORE NURSE COL
FIRSTLADIES ONO
ETNA EPIC FLIP
STATEPOLICE
ELDEST TARO
SLOOP HANGOVER
HERO MOOGS RAVE
OVERHANG SINEW
DICE LETTER
POLICESTATE
ERIE IRMA LOIS
TAN LADIESFIRST
ATE ABETS ESTEE
LES CADET UPSET

52

PERU DRAG UNCAP
CROP IONE NEHRU
SAYBYEBYE DWELL
ROOTS SSE REL
PROWLS NEARMISS
LOG KOKO CPU
ELEV DOTE ASSES
AFRICANAMERICAN
DESTE ASIP CORE
ARM TRIM OLE
APPLEPIE TAMPER
FRO MSN KORAN
LINGO DONMCLEAN
ADDON IDEE ECHO
TESTY ADES SKAT

53

SONAR ATSEA USO
ATARI DUMPY TAR
FIREANDRAIN OVA
ESCALATOR SPAN
COWTIPPING
CAUSAL RELATE
ORRIN BEWARE
DINNERETIQUETTE
AMIDST SNOOK
STATIC LESSEE
CHURCHLADY
YOGA IRONSIDES
TRU OPENINGBELL
HAS USUAL TEASE
EXT RITZY STRAW

54

SLAM BAMA GAIN
CAPO SALON ONTO
OMAN ALERT AJAR
TECTONICPLATE
INHERE HER LOP
ATE ALTA RESIDE
FLYINGSAUCER
ALOE EGO MAST
FIFAWORLDCUP
RAFTED ESAS CHI
ORS ADS PEAHEN
HOLLYWOODBOWL
FLOP ORION OKIE
DARE TITHE VENT
AXED SASS ERGS

55

JANETS LABRAT
INAHEAP FEBREZE
MARSALA APROPOS
STP KEA
PSST SABER MGMT
AHYES DAD MAYER
JUNCTION SIERRA
ATE JACKSON AIG
MORMON JULIETTE
AUGIE JON STEED
STYX COBRA EDDY
NON ORE
SEPHORA OCTOMOM
NOVOTES FERTILE
LECTER DECLAW

56

```
S I O N | V I L E | C A S C A
E N N E | C R U X | R U T H S
A S T A | H O N E | E N R O L
S H O P P I N G C E N T E R |
T A P | E P I | U S N | A T E
A P O R T | C A T T A C K L E
R E F O R M | M O E | A Y E S
| B I T T E R E N D |
A S T I | F O E | M Y R I A D
S H I N G U A R D | L E N T O
H O E | O J S | I D O | A L I
| W I C H I T A L I N E M A N
C I N C O | E L A N | G O N G
L E T E M | R O T E | G O T O
E R O D E | S T E R | S D A K
```

57

```
U M P S | O H A R A | M Y R A
S I R E | A M B E R | P E E P
U S E D | F O S T E R H O M E
R E M A P | E A U | M A X
P R I N C I P A L | S C A R E
E L S | S T I L L | S I N K S
D Y E S | S N L | A I R
| S U M M E R P L A C E |
P I E | I I I | A L E S
W I R E S | M S N B C | O N E
I N E R T | R E S I D E N C E
I S P | E S T | S A G A S
F I E L D H O U S E | T A R O
I D L E | O A S I S | E T T U
T E S T | O D O R S | N E A T
```

58

```
M I M I C | M U S T | S H I P
E V I T A | O S H A | P I S A
M A K E R B R E A K | A T T U
O N E M O R E | G E R I T O L
| M E L T | S A N E |
F I B B E R | R I O T | R H O
A L O U D | G E N U S | M A N
L I O N | S L A N T | D I R K
C A M | S T U D S | P O S S E
O D E | C A M O | S L O S H Y
| R O O T | N A P A |
R E B A T E S | M U S T A R D
A B U T | L O V E R M O N E Y
G O S H | A L A N | A B O D E
A N T S | W E L D | S Y N O D
```

59

```
O C A L A | E R G S | T H E N
C I V I L | R I L E | E A S Y
H E A V Y M E T A L | A S A P
E R S E | E S T D | A P H I D
R A T C H E T | H I M O M |
| H A K U N A M A T A T A
A R H A T | I N A T | R O M
S E A T | H A N D M | W K R P
C P U | B A N O | B O S O M
H O T E L M A N A G E R |
| M N E M E | S M E L L E D
F J O R D | R O T A | D O N E
L E N O | H O R A C E M A N N
A D D L | U B E R | R A D I I
K I E L | M E M E | E P S O M
```

60

```
B A L M | M A T E | B O W I E
A L O E | A V I D | A D H O C
B O O M E R A N G | D E A T H
E F F O R T | T E A K | M A O
S T A R L I T | S P A S M |
| Y E A R S | P R A Y T O
T A B | N A P E | M A B E L
S T A R T S W I T H A B A N G
A R M O R | L E T O | R D A
R A B I E S | L A T C H |
| O L S E N | S T R A N G E
E M O | P E E R | O U I O U I
P I Z Z A | P O W D E R K E G
I S L E S | A M I D | D I S H
C O E N S | L A Z Y | O A S T
```

61

```
R A L L Y . P A P A . B E A R
A V O I D . R I O T . A N N A
T O R E S T O R E S A N I T Y
S I R S . O M B . T R A D E S
. R E T R O . A L U M . . . .
. . O A F . L A D Y L U C K .
N B A . T A I L S . A R E A .
C O L B E R T . S T E W A R T
A R T E . S T O R M . L A Y .
A N A T H E M A . E M B . . .
. . A L E G . M A R C H . . .
S T A N Z A . T W O . I H O P
T O K E E P F E A R A L I V E
A R I A . S E A R . A L T E R
B E N T . E M M Y . R O A R K
```

62

```
A N G . I Z O D . O P P O S E
T O E . N O I R . D O E S O K
H D L . K O L A . E S T A T E
R E A L I T Y B I T E S . . .
O A T E N . . L O I T E R S .
B L O O D B A N K . D O P E Y
. . . . L O U . G O R I E R .
. P A I N I N T H E N E C K .
K I D N A P . R U R . . . . .
P L A N T . B A T M O B I L E
H E R O I N E . . R I G O R .
. . C O U N T D R A C U L A .
L E G E N D . A D I N . E I S
A D O N A I . F A N G . S T E
T O O T L E . T Y K E . S A D
```

63

```
S T O I C . P I N U P . K F C
S W I R L . A N D R E . E R E
W A L K I N G C A N E . Y I N
. . S Q U E A K . P A B S T .
S P R O U T S . S H E I K S .
T H A M E S . F A V O R S . .
A L I E . A R P E L . C O G .
L O S . C O C A I N E . A G O
L X I . O R A N G . B Y R D .
. N I M I T Z . B O R N E O .
R A G T A G . D O P I E S T .
E X C O N . S T O N E S . . .
A L A . C I T I Z E N K A N E
P E I . H A U T E . E L D E R
S S N . E N D O N . R Y D E R
```

64

```
B B S . I B M P C . A T O M
E L O . R A T I O . M A K O
D U D E R A N C H . B R O W
E T O N . K O D I A K S . .
W H I T E R U S S I A N . .
. S K I S . T A N T E S . .
A R I . C E E S . C I A O .
P A R D O N M Y F R E N C H
O B O E . E N D O . O H O .
P E N P A L . C I N Q . . .
. J U L I U S C A E S A R .
A L A T E E N . I A G O . .
K I W I . D R E S S I N G S
I D E E . T E V Y E . D I E
N O D S . O P A R T . Y E S
```

65

```
B O T H . F I T . N E V A D A
I N N O T I M E . U N I S E X
N E T P R O F S . C O S I N E
. . O E R . T E L . T A T S .
. T E N N E S S E E T A N S .
P A L . T L C . L I E . . . .
A B E T . L A M . A S T R O .
N O V I S O R S A L L O W E D
E R E C T . N C O . T O G O .
. A I G . T W P . A I R . . .
. L E A R N E R S P E R M S .
B A R B . J O E . I R A . . .
E U R O P E . C U T I T O U T
E R O D E S . U N C L E L E O
P A R E N T . R A H . R A Y S
```

66

WOODY · BEA · MATCH
ASIRECALL · STOLA
RADIODAYS · ROMAS
· · MISSTEP · CST
ALICE · ION · BASE
RAMON · MANHATTAN
AMAH · KAN · AWW ·
BANANAS · SLEEPER
· BAT · ANO · LALA
ANNIEHALL · AVION
AOUT · IDI · ZELIG
ANC · PERGOLA · ·
MOLTO · INTERIORS
ANEAR · FEBRILITY
POINT · TDS · ALLEN

67

CAJUN · LIP · PAST
ORATE · AMA · ACMES
LIKED · SHIPSHAPE
EDEN · PEERAT · REA
· SHARPSHOOTER
ARTIES · · RAM
SHELLSHOCK · FOBS
CEL · PARTIII · NEA
HALT · SHORTSHEET
· MOO · ELAYNE
SHEEPSHEARER
YAM · THORNS · DAZE
SHOESHINE · SHREW
TARSI · SIR · SACRE
· SEEN · TEA · ETHOS

68

IRAQ · MAPLE · RINK
NANU · IWILL · OMAN
CHIEFTEXAN · APSE
· MEET · MISDEAL
STAGE · GIANTBILL
EAT · LAUD · OIL
RBIS · BIOS · LOCOS
FOOTBALLMATCHUP
SONAR · TIER · KATE
· GYM · ZACH · MIA
JETPACKER · UPPER
ARRANGE · PLEA
ROAR · RAMCHARGER
EDIT · ACRID · INFO
DENY · WHIGS · LEGO

69

JADE · OSHA · WASNT
APOP · RATS · ALTAR
YPSILANTI · REATA
· CALYPSOMUSIC
ACT · ILO · VOTIVE
GOAWRY · SLAV · SER
AMMO · COOLIO
· APOCALYPSENOW
· FAMOUS · ENID
ATV · LUTZ · KPDUTY
SHAWLS · LAI · SHE
SECRETAGENTS
USAIR · GYPSYMOTH
CENTI · AREA · OWIE
HATED · ROWS · GENX

70

JETS · RISEN · MAP
ATOP · RETINA · ILL
NETEARNINGS · NBA
· ESSEN · SLEET
SCUDS · WASTEAREA
CASSIO · HORN
ADO · GRADER · ASAP
DEFINITEARTICLE
STAN · OSIRIS · ULT
· ISLE · DEBBIE
WYATTEARP · TRANS
HESSE · ERASE
ELK · PLANETEARTH
ALE · POMELO · SURE
TOW · EXPEL · TEAR

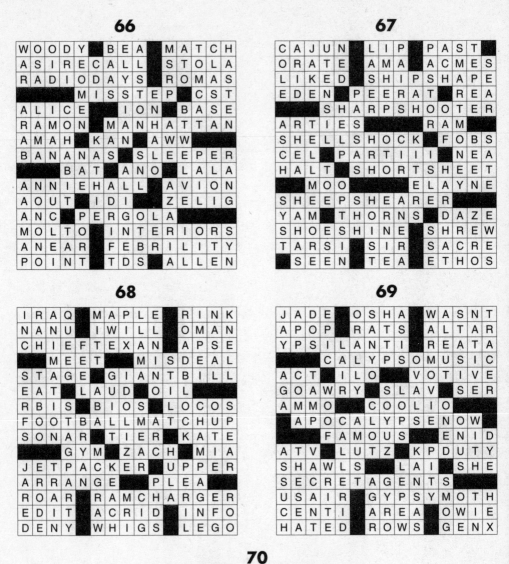

71

```
MORAL ■ PEW ■ CHESS
ELOPE ■ ODE ■ LEGAL
SELES ■ WILLINGLY
HOLDTHEFLOOR ■
■ AURIST ■ YEA
■ HITTHECEILING
MINE ■ DETOX ■ RET
OTHERS ■ NIKONS
PEA ■ POSSE ■ ALTO
■ CLIMBTHEWALLS ■
■ HEC ■ BEARER
■ EXERCISEROOM
SUNSTROKE ■ NORMA
ONAIR ■ ILS ■ ATEAT
DONNA ■ DET ■ SHONE
```

72

```
KITH ■ FLEX ■ ATBAY
ABRA ■ LAVE ■ SHUTE
NOIR ■ ODIN ■ SERTA
JOCKFULLONUTS ■
IKE ■ ONES ■ AMATOL
■ TLC ■ WIE ■ ORA
JEERLEADER ■ SPIT
ALLEY ■ QUE ■ SCENT
MITE ■ JUMPCHANGE
USO ■ MIA ■ HAM ■
PENPAL ■ GLAD ■ STP
■ JESTPROTECTOR
BRONC ■ OORT ■ ALPO
ETHNO ■ PUCE ■ PEAL
TENET ■ STAR ■ OOZE
```

73

```
LEAP ■ MCCOO ■ REST
OSLO ■ ARAIL ■ OTTO
CATSCRADLE ■ THAI
HUSTLING ■ QUILL
■ MONKEYSUNCLE
MRHANEY ■ ATAD
BEENE ■ ADA ■ AFAR
AMA ■ DOGSAGE ■ ACE
SOLO ■ ZAP ■ ZAIRE
■ SEMI ■ UMPIRED
ELEPHANTSEAR ■
PEARS ■ REASSIGN
SORE ■ LIONSSHARE
ONLY ■ ARIEL ■ OGOD
MESS ■ PASTY ■ WOWS
```

74

```
REACT ■ OPTED ■ TIN
ALLAH ■ LLANO ■ HBO
PLANEBOARDS ■ ISM
TEN ■ KERN ■ ASSES
■ MINDBLOGGING
SECANT ■ ODETS ■
PLANK ■ EREI ■ TBA
CHRISTMASCLAROS
AIR ■ YENS ■ AMUSE
■ YEARN ■ ICIEST
BLOTTEDWATER ■
LANCE ■ ITAR ■ ILE
ORB ■ ADAMSLANDER
OVA ■ SNAPE ■ TILES
MAG ■ EASYA ■ EXERT
```

75

```
FAVOR ■ PALM ■ OTIS
READE ■ ASIA ■ OHNO
OILED ■ CHER ■ LEFT
GOODTIME ■ SNAFU ■
SUR ■ ANA ■ ABELARD
■ FINN ■ LARAMIE
SMALLS ■ CERF ■ IAT
CADY ■ ONE ■ ALTE
ACA ■ BTEN ■ SPRYER
LAYDOWN ■ SURF ■
ARSENIO ■ PLO ■ FRO
■ TWEEN ■ YOURHEAD
SHOR ■ KHAN ■ AERIE
PURE ■ LUNG ■ TEAMO
ARKS ■ EDGY ■ ALLIN
```